A PORTRAIT OF THE ARTIST AS A YOUNG MAN

James Joyce

This edition published by Spark Publishing

Spark Publishing
A Division of SparkNotes LLC
120 Fifth Avenue, 8th Floor
New York, NY 10011

Printed and bound in the United States

ISBN 1-58663-388-0

INTRODUCTION: STOPPING TO BUY SPARKNOTES ON A SNOWY EVENING

Whose words these are you *think* you know.
Your paper's due tomorrow, though;
We're glad to see you stopping here
To get some help before you go.

Lost your course? You'll find it here.
Face tests and essays without fear.
Between the words, good grades at stake:
Get great results throughout the year.

Once school bells caused your heart to quake
As teachers circled each mistake.
Use SparkNotes and no longer weep,
Ace every single test you take.

Yes, books are lovely, dark, and deep,
But only what you grasp you keep,
With hours to go before you sleep,
With hours to go before you sleep.

CONTENTS

CONTEXT

J AMES JOYCE WAS BORN on February 2, 1882, in the town of Rathgar, near Dublin, Ireland. He was the oldest of ten children born to a well-meaning but financially inept father and a solemn, pious mother. Joyce's parents managed to scrape together enough money to send their talented son to the Clongowes Wood College, a prestigious boarding school, and then to Belvedere College, where Joyce excelled as an actor and writer. Later, he attended University College in Dublin, where he became increasingly committed to language and literature as a champion of Modernism. In 1902, Joyce left the university and moved to Paris, but briefly returned to Ireland in 1903 upon the death of his mother. Shortly after his mother's death, Joyce began work on the story that would later become *A Portrait of the Artist as a Young Man.*

Published in serial form in 1914–1915, *A Portrait of the Artist as a Young Man* draws on many details from Joyce's early life. The novel's protagonist, Stephen Dedalus, is in many ways Joyce's fictional double—Joyce had even published stories under the pseudonym "Stephen Daedalus" before writing the novel. Like Joyce himself, Stephen is the son of an impoverished father and a highly devout Catholic mother. Also like Joyce, he attends Clongowes Wood, Belvedere, and University Colleges, struggling with questions of faith and nationality before leaving Ireland to make his own way as an artist. Many of the scenes in the novel are fictional, but some of its most powerful moments are autobiographical: both the Christmas dinner scene and Stephen's first sexual experience with the Dublin prostitute closely resemble actual events in Joyce's life.

In addition to drawing heavily on Joyce's personal life, *A Portrait of the Artist as a Young Man* also makes a number of references to the politics and religion of early-twentieth-century Ireland. When Joyce was growing up, Ireland had been under British rule since the sixteenth century, and tensions between Ireland and Britain had been especially high since the potato blight of 1845. There was considerable religious tension: the majority of Irish, including the Joyces, were Catholics, and favored Irish independence. The Protestant minority mostly wished to remain united with Britain.

Around the time Joyce was born, the Irish nationalist Charles Stewart Parnell was spearheading the movement for Irish independence. In 1890, however, Parnell's longstanding affair with a married woman was exposed, leading the Catholic Church to condemn him and causing many of his former followers to turn against him. Many Irish nationalists blamed Parnell's death, which occurred only a year later, on the Catholic Church. Indeed, we see these strong opinions about Parnell surface in *A Portrait of the Artist as a Young Man* during an emotional Christmas dinner argument among members of the Dedalus family. By 1900, the Irish people felt largely united in demanding freedom from British rule. In *A Portrait of the Artist as a Young Man*, Stephen's friends at University College frequently confront him with political questions about the struggle between Ireland and England.

After completing *A Portrait of the Artist as a Young Man* in Zurich in 1915, Joyce returned to Paris, where he wrote two more major novels, *Ulysses* and *Finnegans Wake,* over the course of the next several years. These three novels, along with a short story collection, *Dubliners,* form the core of his remarkable literary career. He died in 1941.

Today, Joyce is celebrated as one of the great literary pioneers of the twentieth century. He was one of the first writers to make extensive and convincing use of stream of consciousness, a stylistic form in which written prose seeks to represent the characters' stream of inner thoughts and perceptions rather than render these characters from an objective, external perspective. This technique, used in *A Portrait of the Artist as a Young Man* mostly during the opening sections and in Chapter 5, sometimes makes for difficult reading. With effort, however, the seemingly jumbled perceptions of the stream of consciousness narration can crystallize into a coherent and sophisticated portrayal of a character's experience.

Another stylistic technique for which Joyce is noted is the epiphany, a moment in which a character makes a sudden, profound realization—whether prompted by an external object or a voice from within—that creates a change in his or her perception of the world. Joyce uses epiphany most notably in *Dubliners,* but *A Portrait of the Artist as a Young Man* is full of these sudden moments of spiritual revelation as well. Most notable is a scene in which Stephen sees a young girl wading at the beach, which strikes him with the sudden realization that an appreciation of beauty can be truly good. This moment is a classic example of Joyce's belief that an epiphany can dramatically alter the human spirit in a matter of just a few seconds.

PLOT OVERVIEW

A PORTRAIT OF THE ARTIST AS A YOUNG MAN tells the story of Stephen Dedalus, a boy growing up in Ireland at the end of the nineteenth century, as he gradually decides to cast off all his social, familial, and religious constraints to live a life devoted to the art of writing. As a young boy, Stephen's Catholic faith and Irish nationality heavily influence him. He attends a strict religious boarding school called Clongowes Wood College. At first, Stephen is lonely and homesick at the school, but as time passes he finds his place among the other boys. He enjoys his visits home, even though family tensions run high after the death of the Irish political leader Charles Stewart Parnell. This sensitive subject becomes the topic of a furious, politically charged argument over the family's Christmas dinner.

Stephen's father, Simon, is inept with money, and the family sinks deeper and deeper into debt. After a summer spent in the company of his Uncle Charles, Stephen learns that the family cannot afford to send him back to Clongowes, and that they will instead move to Dublin. Stephen starts attending a prestigious day school called Belvedere, where he grows to excel as a writer and as an actor in the student theater. His first sexual experience, with a young Dublin prostitute, unleashes a storm of guilt and shame in Stephen, as he tries to reconcile his physical desires with the stern Catholic morality of his surroundings. For a while, he ignores his religious upbringing, throwing himself with debauched abandon into a variety of sins—masturbation, gluttony, and more visits to prostitutes, among others. Then, on a three-day religious retreat, Stephen hears a trio of fiery sermons about sin, judgment, and hell. Deeply shaken, the young man resolves to rededicate himself to a life of Christian piety.

Stephen begins attending Mass every day, becoming a model of Catholic piety, abstinence, and self-denial. His religious devotion is so pronounced that the director of his school asks him to consider entering the priesthood. After briefly considering the offer, Stephen realizes that the austerity of the priestly life is utterly incompatible with his love for sensual beauty. That day, Stephen learns from his sister that the family will be moving, once again for financial reasons. Anxiously awaiting news about his acceptance to the university, Stephen goes for a walk on the beach, where he observes a young girl wading in the tide. He is struck by her beauty, and realizes, in a moment of epiphany, that the love and desire of beauty should not be a source of shame. Stephen resolves to live his life to the fullest, and vows not to be constrained by the boundaries of his family, his nation, and his religion.

Stephen moves on to the university, where he develops a number of strong friendships, and is especially close with a young man named Cranly. In a series of conversations with his companions, Stephen works to formulate his theories about art. While he is dependent on his friends as listeners, he is also determined to create an independent existence, liberated from the expectations of friends and family. He becomes more and more determined to free himself from all limiting pressures, and eventually decides to leave Ireland to escape them. Like his namesake, the mythical Daedalus, Stephen hopes to build himself wings on which he can fly above all obstacles and achieve a life as an artist.

CHARACTER LIST

Stephen Dedalus The main character of *A Portrait of the Artist as a Young Man*. Growing up, Stephen goes through long phases of hedonism and deep religiosity. He eventually adopts a philosophy of aestheticism, greatly valuing beauty and art. Stephen is essentially Joyce's alter ego, and many of the events of Stephen's life mirror events from Joyce's own youth.

Simon Dedalus Stephen's father, an impoverished former medical student with a strong sense of Irish patriotism. Sentimental about his past, Simon Dedalus frequently reminisces about his youth.

Mary Dedalus Stephen's mother and Simon Dedalus's wife. Mary is very religious, and argues with her son about attending religious services.

The Dedalus children Though his siblings do not play a major role in the novel, Stephen has several brothers and sisters, including Maurice, Katey, Maggie, and Boody.

Emma Clery Stephen's beloved, the young girl to whom he is fiercely attracted over the course of many years. Stephen constructs Emma as an ideal of femininity, even though he does not know her well.

Mr. John Casey Simon Dedalus's friend, who attends the Christmas dinner at which young Stephen is allowed to sit with the adults for the first time. Like Simon, Mr. Casey is a staunch Irish nationalist, and at the dinner he argues with Dante over the fate of Parnell.

Charles Stewart Parnell An Irish political leader who is not an actual character in the novel, but whose death touches many of its characters. Parnell had powerfully led the Irish National Party until he was condemned for having an affair with a married woman.

Dante   (Mrs. Riordan) The extremely fervent and piously Catholic governess of the Dedalus children. Dante, whose real name is Mrs. Riordan, becomes involved in a long and unpleasant argument with Mr. Casey over the fate of Parnell during Christmas dinner.

Uncle Charles Stephen's lively great uncle. Charles lives with Stephen's family. During the summer, the young Stephen enjoys taking long walks with his uncle and listening to Charles and Simon discuss the history of both Ireland and the Dedalus family.

Eileen Vance A young girl who lives near Stephen when he is a young boy. When Stephen tells Dante that he wants to marry Eileen, Dante is enraged because Eileen is a Protestant.

Father Conmee The rector at Clongowes Wood College, where Stephen attends school as a young boy.

Father Dolan The cruel prefect of studies at Clongowes Wood College.

Wells   The bully at Clongowes. Wells taunts Stephen for kissing his mother before he goes to bed, and one day he pushes Stephen into a filthy cesspool, causing Stephen to catch a bad fever.

Athy   A friendly boy whom Stephen meets in the infirmary at Clongowes. Athy likes Stephen Dedalus because they both have unusual names.

Brother Michael The kindly cleric who tends to Stephen and Athy in the Clongowes infirmary after Wells pushes Stephen into the cesspool.

Fleming   One of Stephen's friends at Clongowes.

Dean of Studies A Jesuit priest at University College.

Johnny Cashman A friend of Simon Dedalus.

Father Arnall Stephen's stern Latin teacher at Clongowes. Later, when Stephen is at Belvedere College, Father Arnall delivers a series of lectures on death and hell that have a profound influence on Stephen.

Mike Flynn A friend of Simon Dedalus's who tries, with little success, to train Stephen to be a runner during their summer at Blackrock.

Aubrey Mills A young boy with whom Stephen plays imaginary adventure games at Blackrock.

Vincent Heron A rival of Stephen's at Belvedere.

Boland and Nash Two schoolmates of Stephen's at Belvedere, who taunt and bully him.

Cranly   Stephen's best friend at the university, in whom he confides his thoughts and feelings. In this sense, Cranly represents a secular confessor for Stephen. Eventually, Cranly begins to encourage Stephen to conform to the wishes of his family and to try harder to fit in with his peers—advice that Stephen fiercely resents.

Davin   Another of Stephen's friends at the university. Davin comes from the Irish provinces and has a simple, solid nature. Stephen admires his talent for athletics, but disagrees with his unquestioning Irish patriotism, which Davin encourages Stephen to adopt.

Lynch   Another of Stephen's friends at the university, a coarse and often unpleasantly dry young man. Lynch is poorer than Stephen. Stephen explains his theory of aesthetics to Lynch in Chapter 5.

McCann   A fiercely political student at the university who tries to convince Stephen to be more concerned with politics.

Temple   A young man at the university who openly admires Stephen's keen independence and tries to copy his ideas and sentiments.

ANALYSIS OF MAJOR CHARACTERS

STEPHEN DEDALUS

Modeled after Joyce himself, Stephen is a sensitive, thoughtful boy who reappears in Joyce's later masterpiece, *Ulysses*. In *A Portrait of the Artist as a Young Man*, though Stephen's large family runs into deepening financial difficulties, his parents manage to send him to prestigious schools and eventually to a university. As he grows up, Stephen grapples with his nationality, religion, family, and morality, and finally decides to reject all socially imposed bonds and instead live freely as an artist.

Stephen undergoes several crucial transformations over the course of the novel. The first, which occurs during his first years at Clongowes, is from a sheltered little boy to a bright student who understands social interactions and can begin to make sense of the world around him. The second, which occurs when Stephen sleeps with the Dublin prostitute, is from innocence to debauchery. The third, which occurs when Stephen hears Father Arnall's speech on death and hell, is from an unrepentant sinner to a devout Catholic. Finally, Stephen's greatest transformation is from near fanatical religiousness to a new devotion to art and beauty. This transition takes place in Chapter 4, when he is offered entry to the Jesuit order but refuses it in order to attend university. Stephen's refusal and his subsequent epiphany on the beach mark his transition from belief in God to belief in aesthetic beauty. This transformation continues through his college years. By the end of his time in college, Stephen has become a fully formed artist, and his diary entries reflect the independent individual he has become.

SIMON DEDALUS

Simon Dedalus spends a great deal of his time reliving past experiences, lost in his own sentimental nostalgia. Joyce often uses Simon to symbolize the bonds and burdens that Stephen's family and nationality place upon him as he grows up. Simon is a nostalgic, tragic figure: he has a deep pride in tradition, but he is unable to keep his own affairs in order. To Stephen, his father Simon represents the parts of family, nation, and tradition that hold him back, and against which he feels he must rebel. The closest look we get at Simon is on the visit to Cork with Stephen, during which Simon gets drunk and sentimentalizes about his past. Joyce paints a picture of a man who has ruined himself and, instead of facing his problems, drowns them in alcohol and nostalgia.

EMMA CLERY

Emma is Stephen's "beloved," the young girl to whom he is intensely attracted over the course of many years. Stephen does not know Emma particularly well, and is generally too embarrassed or afraid to talk to her, but feels a powerful response stirring within him whenever he sees her. Stephen's first poem, "To E— C—," is written to Emma. She is a shadowy figure throughout the novel, and we know almost nothing about her even at the novel's end. For Stephen, Emma symbolizes one end of a spectrum of femininity. Stephen seems able to perceive only the extremes of this spectrum: for him, women are either pure, distant, and unapproachable, like Emma, or impure, sexual, and common, like the prostitutes he visits during his time at Belvedere.

CHARLES STEWART PARNELL

Parnell is not fictional, and does not actually appear as a character in the novel. However, as an Irish political leader, he is a polarizing figure whose death influences many characters in *A Portrait of the Artist as a Young Man*. During the late nineteenth century, Parnell had been the powerful leader of the Irish National Party, and his influence seemed to promise Irish independence from England. When Parnell's affair with a married woman was exposed, however, he was condemned by the Catholic Church and fell from grace. His fevered attempts to regain his former position of influence contributed to his death from exhaustion. Many people in Ireland, such as the character of John Casey in Joyce's novel, considered Parnell a hero and blamed the church for his death. Many others, such as the character Dante, thought the church was correct in condemning Parnell. These disputes over Parnell's character are at the root of the bitter and abusive argument that erupts during the Dedalus family's

Christmas dinner when Stephen is still a young boy. In this sense, Parnell represents the burden of Irish nationality that Stephen comes to believe is preventing him from realizing himself as an artist.

CRANLY

Stephen's best friend at the university, Cranly also acts as a kind of nonreligious confessor for Stephen. In long, late-night talks, Stephen tells Cranly everything, just as he used to tell the priests everything during his days of religious fervor. While Cranly is a good friend to Stephen, he does not understand Stephen's need for absolute freedom. Indeed, to Cranly, leaving behind all the trappings of society would be terribly lonely. It is this difference that separates the true artist, Stephen, from the artist's friend, Cranly. In that sense, Cranly represents the nongenius, a young man who is not called to greatness as Stephen is, and who therefore does not have to make the same sacrifices.

CHARACTER ANALYSIS

THEMES, MOTIFS & SYMBOLS

THEMES

Themes are the fundamental and often universal ideas explored in a literary work.

THE DEVELOPMENT OF INDIVIDUAL CONSCIOUSNESS

Perhaps the most famous aspect of *A Portrait of the Artist as a Young Man* is Joyce's innovative use of stream of consciousness, a style in which the author directly transcribes the thoughts and sensations that go through a character's mind, rather than simply describing those sensations from the external standpoint of an observer. Joyce's use of stream of consciousness makes *A Portrait of the Artist as a Young Man* a story of the development of Stephen's mind. In the first chapter, the very young Stephen is only capable of describing his world in simple words and phrases. The sensations that he experiences are all jumbled together with a child's lack of attention to cause and effect. Later, when Stephen is a teenager obsessed with religion, he is able to think in a clearer, more adult manner. Paragraphs are more logically ordered than in the opening sections of the novel, and thoughts progress logically. Stephen's mind is more mature and he is now more coherently aware of his surroundings. Nonetheless, he still trusts blindly in the church, and his passionate emotions of guilt and religious ecstasy are so strong that they get in the way of rational thought. It is only in the final chapter, when Stephen is at the university, that he seems truly rational. By the end of the novel, Joyce renders a portrait of a mind that has achieved emotional, intellectual, and artistic adulthood.

The development of Stephen's consciousness in *A Portrait of the Artist as a Young Man* is particularly interesting because, insofar as Stephen is a portrait of Joyce himself, Stephen's development gives us insight into the development of a literary genius. Stephen's experiences hint at the influences that transformed Joyce himself into the great writer he is considered today: Stephen's obsession with language; his strained relations with religion, family, and culture; and his dedication to forging an aesthetic of his own mirror the ways in which Joyce related to the various tensions in his life during his formative years. In the last chapter of the novel, we also learn that genius, though in many ways a calling, also requires great work and considerable sacrifice. Watching Stephen's daily struggle to puzzle out his aesthetic philosophy, we get a sense of the great task that awaits him.

THE PITFALLS OF RELIGIOUS EXTREMISM

Brought up in a devout Catholic family, Stephen initially ascribes to an absolute belief in the morals of the church. As a teenager, this belief leads him to two opposite extremes, both of which are harmful. At first, he falls into the extreme of sin, repeatedly sleeping with prostitutes and deliberately turning his back on religion. Though Stephen sins willfully, he is always aware that he acts in violation of the church's rules. Then, when Father Arnall's speech prompts him to return to Catholicism, he bounces to the other extreme, becoming a perfect, near fanatical model of religious devotion and obedience. Eventually, however, Stephen realizes that both of these lifestyles—the completely sinful and the completely devout—are extremes that have been false and harmful. He does not want to lead a completely debauched life, but also rejects austere Catholicism because he feels that it does not permit him the full experience of being human. Stephen ultimately reaches a decision to embrace life and celebrate humanity after seeing a young girl wading at a beach. To him, the girl is a symbol of pure goodness and of life lived to the fullest.

THE ROLE OF THE ARTIST

A Portrait of the Artist as a Young Man explores what it means to become an artist. Stephen's decision at the end of the novel—to leave his family and friends behind and go into exile in order to become an artist—suggests that Joyce sees the artist as a necessarily isolated figure. In his decision, Stephen turns his back on his community, refusing to accept the constraints of political involvement, religious devotion, and family commitment that the community places on its members.

However, though the artist is an isolated figure, Stephen's ultimate goal is to give a voice to the very community that he is leaving. In the last few lines of the novel, Stephen expresses his desire to "forge in the smithy of my soul the uncreated conscience of my race." He recognizes that his community will always be a part of him, as it has created and shaped his identity. When he creatively expresses his own ideas, he will also convey the voice of his entire community. Even as Stephen turns his back on the traditional forms of participation and membership in a community, he envisions his writing as a service to the community.

THE NEED FOR IRISH AUTONOMY

Despite his desire to steer clear of politics, Stephen constantly ponders Ireland's place in the world. He concludes that the Irish have always been a subservient people, allowing outsiders to control them. In his conversation with the dean of studies at the university, he realizes that even the language of the Irish people really belongs to the English. Stephen's perception of Ireland's subservience has two effects on his development as an artist. First, it makes him determined to escape the bonds that his Irish ancestors have accepted. As we see in his conversation with Davin, Stephen feels an anxious need to emerge from his Irish heritage as his own person, free from the shackles that have traditionally confined his country: "Do you fancy I am going to pay in my own life and person debts they made?" Second, Stephen's perception makes him determined to use his art to reclaim autonomy for Ireland. Using the borrowed language of English, he plans to write in a style that will be both autonomous from England and true to the Irish people.

MOTIFS

Motifs are recurring structures, contrasts, or literary devices that can help to develop and inform the text's major themes.

MUSIC

Music, especially singing, appears repeatedly throughout *A Portrait of the Artist as a Young Man*. Stephen's appreciation of music is closely tied to his love for the sounds of language. As a young child, he turns Dante's threats into a song, " [A]pologise, pull out his eyes, pull out his eyes, apologise." Singing is more than just language—it is language transformed by vibrant humanity. Music appeals to the part of Stephen that wants to live life to the fullest. We see this aspect of music near the end of the novel, when Stephen suddenly feels at peace upon hearing a woman singing. Her voice prompts him to recall his resolution to leave Ireland and become a writer, reinforcing his determination to celebrate life through writing.

MOTIFS

FLIGHT

Stephen Dedalus's very name embodies the idea of flight. Stephen's namesake, Daedalus, is a figure from Greek mythology, a renowned craftsman who designs the famed Labyrinth of Crete for King Minos. Minos keeps Daedalus and his son, Icarus, imprisoned on Crete, but Daedalus makes plans to escape by using feathers, twine, and wax to fashion a set of wings for himself and his son. Daedalus escapes successfully, but Icarus flies too high. The sun's heat melts the wax holding Icarus's wings together, and he plummets to his death in the sea.

In the context of *A Portrait of the Artist as a Young Man*, we can see Stephen as representative of both Daedalus and Icarus, as Stephen's father also has the last name of Dedalus. With this mythological reference, Joyce implies that Stephen must always balance his desire to flee Ireland with the danger of overestimating his own abilities—the intellectual equivalent of Icarus's flight too close to the sun. To diminish the dangers of attempting too much too soon, Stephen bides his time at the university, developing his aesthetic theory fully before attempting to leave Ireland and write seriously. The birds that appear to Stephen in the third section of Chapter 5 signal that it is finally time for Stephen, now fully formed as an artist, to take flight himself.

PRAYERS, SECULAR SONGS, AND LATIN PHRASES

We can often tell Stephen's state of mind by looking at the fragments of prayers, songs, and Latin phrases that Joyce inserts into the text. When Stephen is a schoolboy, Joyce includes childish, sincere prayers that mirror the manner in which a child might devoutly believe in the church, even without understanding the meaning of its religious doctrine. When Stephen prays in church despite the fact that he has committed a mortal sin, Joyce transcribes a long passage of the Latin prayer, but it is clear that Stephen merely speaks the words without believing them. Then, when Stephen is at the university, Latin is used as a joke—his friends translate colloquial phrases like "peace over the whole bloody globe" into Latin because they find the academic sound of the translation amusing. This jocular use of Latin mocks both the young men's education and the stern, serious manner in which Latin is used in the church. These linguistic jokes demonstrate that Stephen is no longer serious about religion. Finally, Joyce includes a few lines from the Irish folk song "Rosie O'Grady" near the end of the novel. These simple lines reflect the peaceful feeling that the song brings to Stephen and Cranly, as well as the traditional Irish culture that Stephen plans to leave behind. Throughout the novel, such prayers, songs, and phrases form the background of Stephen's life.

SYMBOLS

Symbols are objects, characters, figures, or colors used to represent abstract ideas or concepts.

GREEN AND MAROON
Stephen associates the colors green and maroon with his governess, Dante, and with two leaders of the Irish resistance, Charles Parnell and Michael Davitt. In a dream after Parnell's death, Stephen sees Dante dressed in green and maroon as the Irish people mourn their fallen leader. This vision indicates that Stephen associates the two colors with the way Irish politics are played out among the members of his own family.

EMMA
Emma appears only in glimpses throughout most of Stephen's young life, and he never gets to know her as a person. Instead, she becomes a symbol of pure love, untainted by sexuality or reality. Stephen worships Emma as the ideal of feminine purity. When he goes through his devoutly religious phase, he imagines his reward for his piety as a union with Emma in heaven. It is only later, when he is at the university, that we finally see a real conversation between Stephen and Emma. Stephen's diary entry regarding this conversation portrays Emma as a real, friendly, and somewhat ordinary girl, but certainly not the goddess Stephen earlier makes her out to be. This more balanced view of Emma mirrors Stephen's abandonment of the extremes of complete sin and complete devotion in favor of a middle path, the devotion to the appreciation of beauty.

Summary & Analysis

Chapter 1, Section 1

Summary

> *Once upon a time and a very good time it was there*
> *was a moocow coming down along the road and this*
> *moocow that was coming down along the road met a*
> *nicens little boy named baby tuckoo. . . .*
>
> (See QUOTATIONS, p. 49)

Stephen's father, Simon Dedalus, tells his young son an old-fashioned children's story. Simon begins the story with the traditional "[o]nce upon a time" and uses babyish words like "moocow." With his childish yet vivid imagination, the young Stephen identifies with the story's character, "baby tuckoo." We see some of Stephen's impressions of early childhood: the cold bed-sheets, the pleasant smell of his mother, the applause he receives from his governess Dante and his Uncle Charles when he dances to the hornpipe.

At one point, Stephen expresses his intention to marry the young girl, Eileen Vance, who lives next door. Eileen happens to be Protestant, however, and in response to his Catholic family's shock, Stephen crawls under the table. Stephen's mother assures the others that he will apologize, and Dante adds a threat that eagles will pull out Stephen's eyes if he does not apologize. Stephen turns these threatening words into a ditty in his mind.

The story shifts to Stephen's experience at Clongowes Wood College. Stephen watches other boys playing ball but does not participate himself. The other boys are mildly antagonistic toward Stephen, asking his name and questioning what kind of a name it is. They ask about Stephen's social rank and want to know whether his father is a magistrate. In class, Stephen is forced to compete in an academic contest in which the opposing teams wear badges with red or white roses—emblems of the noble York and Lancaster families from English history. Stephen does not perform well, and wonders whether green roses are possible.

Stephen tries to study, but instead meditates on himself, God, and the cosmos. He examines his own address written in his geography textbook, beginning with himself and listing his school, city, county, country, and so on in ascending order, ending in "The Universe." Stephen wonders whether the different names for God in different languages refer to the same being, and concludes that the names are in fact all the same being. When the bell rings for night prayers, Stephen addresses God directly. The chaplain's clear and formulaic prayer contrasts with Stephen's own quietly murmured prayer for his family's well-being. Dreading the cold sheets, Stephen climbs into bed and shivers. In a feverish vision, he thinks of a big black dog with bright eyes and of a castle long ago.

Later, various people ask whether Stephen is sick, and we find out that his sickness is probably the result of having been pushed into the "square ditch," or cesspool, the day before. Wells, the boy who pushed Stephen, is the ringleader of the school bullies. Wells had again tormented Stephen by asking whether Stephen kisses his mother. Stephen was unsure whether to answer yes or no, and the boys laughed in both cases anyway.

Stephen's illness enables him to skip class as he recovers in the infirmary. The kind and humorous Brother Michael cares for Stephen, who wonders if he will die from his illness. Stephen tells himself that death indeed might be possible, and he imagines his own funeral. Another student patient in the infirmary, Athy, asks Stephen riddles that he cannot solve. Stephen daydreams about returning home to recover. At the end of the section, Brother Michael announces the death of Parnell, the Irish patriot.

ANALYSIS

Stephen is the hero of *A Portrait of the Artist as a Young Man,* and, in fact, Joyce titled an early version of the novel *Stephen Hero.* The narrative is limited to Stephen's consciousness, so his misperceptions become part of the story—there is no narrator who explains the difference between Stephen's reality and objective reality. Stephen is essentially Joyce's alter ego, and there are many factual similarities between Stephen's life and Joyce's. Clongowes, for example, had been Joyce's boarding school in real life. The novel is more than just an autobiography, however, as Joyce is not merely recounting elements of his own boyhood, but also meditating on what it means to be a young man growing up in a confusing modern world. Stephen's bewilderment about the world and its strange rules reflects the sensation of alienation and confusion that Joyce and a number of his literary peers felt at the beginning of the twentieth century. We see Stephen's alienation on the playground, where he watches other boys playing ball but does not participate himself. Stephen's feeling of being a dissatisfied outsider develops steadily throughout the novel.

The fact that the novel opens with a story emphasizes the importance of art—particularly literary art—in Joyce's world. The fact that the story deeply influences Stephen demonstrates that art is not mere empty entertainment, but has the power to form people's identities and shape their thoughts. Stephen's reaction to the story is to imagine that "[h]e was a baby tuckoo": he becomes conscious of his own existence at this young age by identifying with a character in a fictional story. Similarly, Joyce implies that art can defend against danger or cure wounds. When Stephen is scolded for expressing his wish to marry a Protestant girl, he uses art to soothe his soul, making a song out of his governess's gruesome threat: "Pull out his eyes, / Apologise. . . ." Art also has a political dimension: in the academic competition at Clongowes, the teams take their emblems from the Wars of the Roses. Stephen, however, meditates on the red rose and the white rose only in terms of the fact that "those were beautiful colours to think of." It may seem that Stephen is ignoring politics and history, focusing only on beauty. But this feeling for beauty actually brings Stephen back to history and politics, as he wonders whether a rose could possibly be green, the traditional color of Ireland. With this image of the green rose, Joyce may be slyly hinting at the possibility of an independent Irish state. A sense of beauty may in this regard be quite revolutionary.

One of the most notable features of Stephen's artistic development in this first section is his interest in the sounds of language. Stephen notices sounds even in the very first passages, when he is young enough to use baby words like "moocow" and "tuckoo." When he is a bit older, he ponders the intriguing sound of the word "wine," and imagines that the cricket bats are saying, "pick, pack, pock, puck." This interest in sounds and wordplay reveals much about Joyce himself, who was one of the twentieth century's most important innovators of language. Joyce was also a pioneer in psychological fiction and stream of consciousness technique, capturing the illogical associations made by the human mind and its odd jumps from topic to topic. The montage of perceptions in Stephen's first memories lack traditional realistic description, giving us mental impressions instead, as if thoughts are flowing directly onto the page. Joyce would later refine this stream of consciousness technique to great effect in his novel *Ulysses*.

CHAPTER 1, SECTIONS 2–3

SUMMARY: CHAPTER 1, SECTION 2

The scene shifts to the Dedalus home, where Stephen has returned from boarding school for Christmas vacation. This is the first Christmas dinner during which the young Stephen is allowed to sit at the adult table. The Dedalus family, Dante, Uncle Charles, and a friend of Mr. Dedalus named Mr. Casey are waiting for the food to be brought in. Mr. Dedalus and Mr. Casey chat about an acquaintance who has been manufacturing explosives. The turkey is brought in, and Stephen says grace before the meal.

Mr. Dedalus speaks approvingly of a mutual friend who, by confronting a priest directly, has criticized the involvement of the Catholic Church in Irish politics. Dante strongly disapproves, saying that it is not right for any Catholic to criticize the church. The disagreement soon turns into an angry dispute. Dante quotes the Bible, saying that priests must always be respected. She feels that, as Catholics, it is their duty to follow orders from their priests and bishops without questioning them, even when those orders might be opposed to the Irish patriots' cause.

Stephen watches the dispute with bewilderment, not understanding why anyone would be against priests. He believes Dante is right, but remembers his father criticizing Dante because she used to be a nun. Mr. Casey tells a story of being accosted by an old Catholic woman who had degraded the name of Parnell and the name of the woman with whom Parnell had an adulterous affair. Casey had ended up spitting on the old woman. This anecdote amuses the men but infuriates Dante, who cries that God and religion must come before everything else. Mr. Casey responds that if Dante's words are true, then perhaps Ireland should not have God at all. Dante is enraged and leaves the table, and Mr. Casey weeps for his dead political leader Parnell.

SUMMARY: CHAPTER 1, SECTION 3

Back at school after Christmas vacation, Stephen listens to a muted conversation between Wells and several other students. They are talking about a couple of boys who fled the school for wrongdoing and were later nabbed. Wells believes the boys stole wine from the school's sacristy. The other boys fall silent at the horror of this offense against God.

Athy gives a different account of the boys' crime. He says they were caught "smugging," or engaging in some sort of homosexual play. Stephen reflects on this suggestion, recalling the fine white hands of one of the students, and thinking also of the soft ivory hands of his neighbor Eileen Vance. One boy, Fleming, complains that all the students will be punished for the wrongdoing of two. Fleming suggests that they could mount a rebellion against such an injustice.

The boys are summoned back into the classroom. After the writing lesson, Father Arnall begins the Latin lesson. Fleming is unable to answer a question and the prefect of studies, Father Dolan, pandies him, or lashes his hands. Afterward, the prefect notices that Stephen is not working and demands to know why. Father Arnall tells Father Dolan that Stephen has been excused from class work because his glasses are broken and he cannot see well. Stephen is telling the truth, but the unbelieving prefect pandies him as well.

Later, the boys discuss the incident and urge Stephen to denounce the prefect to the rector. Stephen is reluctant. Finally, he summons the courage to march down the long corridors filled with pictures of saints and martyrs toward the rector's office. Stephen tells the rector what happened, and the rector says he will speak to Father Dolan. When Stephen tells the other boys he has reported on Dolan to the rector, they hoist him over their heads as a hero.

ANALYSIS: CHAPTER 1, SECTIONS 2–3

The Christmas dinner dispute introduces the political landscape of late nineteenth-century Ireland into the novel. This is the first Christmas meal at which Stephen is allowed to sit at the grown-up table, a milestone in his path toward adulthood. The dispute that unfolds among Dante, Mr. Dedalus, and Mr. Casey makes Stephen quickly realize, however, that adulthood is fraught with conflicts, doubts, and anger. This discussion engenders no harmonious Christmas feeling of family togetherness. Rather, the growing boy learns that politics is often such a charged subject that it can cause huge rifts even within a single home.

Dante's tumultuous departure from the dinner table is the first in a pattern of incidents in which characters declare independence and break away from a group for political and ideological reasons. Indeed, the political landscape of Ireland is deeply divided when the action of the novel occurs. Secularists like Mr. Dedalus and Mr. Casey feel that religion is keeping Ireland from progress and independence, while the orthodox, like Dante, feel that religion should take precedence in Irish culture. The secularists consider Parnell the savior of Ireland, but Parnell's shame at being caught in an extramarital affair tarnishes his political luster and earns him the church's condemnation. This condemnation on the part of the church mirrors Stephen's shame over expressing a desire to marry Eileen Vance, who is Protestant. On the whole, however, Stephen's reaction to his family's dispute is sheer bafflement.

These chapters also explore the frequently arbitrary nature of crime and punishment. The fact that the boys in Stephen's class at Clongowes know that they will all be punished for the transgressions of the two caught "smugging" indicates that they are accustomed to unfair retribution. Furthermore, none of the instances of wrongdoing mentioned so far in the novel have been crimes of malice. Stephen when he wishes to marry Eileen. The boys at Clongowes are caught in homosexual activity. Parnell is caught in a relationship with another woman. Yet none of these offenses is motivated by any overt ill will toward others. None of them robs, kills, or wishes harm directly upon another, yet they are all punished more severely than they deserve. Joyce explores this idea of undeserved punishment explicitly when Stephen is painfully punished for a transgression that he has not committed. When Stephen later defends himself and denounces the punishment as unfair, he acts as a representative of all the others who are unfairly punished.

There is great symbolic importance in the scene in which Stephen's peers lift him up over their heads and call him a hero, as it suggests a heroic side of the young boy that we have not seen before. Stephen's summoning of the courage to denounce Father Dolan's injustice is a moral triumph, rather than a more conventional heroic triumph in sports or fighting. Joyce highlights the difference between these two kinds of heroism in the pictures of martyrs that Stephen passes on his way to the rector's office. His walk among the images of upright men suggests that he may be joining their ranks, and his moral victory foreshadows his later ambitions to become a spiritual guide for his country. The role of hero does not necessarily come easily to Stephen, however. His schoolmates lift him up "till he struggled to get free," suggesting that heroism is a burden associated with constraints or a lack of freedom. Significantly, Stephen's heroic role does not ensure any new feeling of social belonging: after the cheers die away, Stephen realizes that he is alone. Joyce implies that becoming a hero may not bring an end to Stephen's outsider status or to his solitude.

CHAPTER 2, SECTIONS 1-2

SUMMARY : CHAPTER 2, SECTION 1

Stephen spends the summer in his family's new house in Blackrock, a town near Dublin. He enjoys the company of his Uncle Charles, a lively old man who smokes horrible "black twists" of tobacco and allows the boy to take handfuls of fruit from a local vendor. Every morning, Stephen and Uncle Charles take a walk through the marketplace to the park, where Stephen meets Mike Flynn, a friend of his father's. Flynn tries to train Stephen to be a runner, but Stephen doubts whether he will ever be very successful. After training, Stephen goes to the chapel with Uncle Charles for morning prayers. Stephen respects his uncle's piety but does not share it.

Stephen takes weekend walks through the town with his father and uncle, listening to their political discussions and their stories about the past. Stephen does not understand many of their references. At home, Stephen reads Alexandre Dumas's novel *The Count of Monte Cristo*, and is deeply engrossed in its adventure and romance. Stephen imagines himself as the lover of Mercédès, the novel's heroine. Ashamed of his father's poor management of the family's finances, Stephen uses the imaginary adventures of Dumas's novel as an escape. He befriends a young boy named Aubrey Mills, who becomes his constant companion in reenacting the adventures of *The Count of Monte Cristo*. Stephen feels that he is different from the other children he knows, and that he is in touch with a higher world. He imagines a future moment in which he will be transfigured by some magic revelation.

SUMMARY: CHAPTER 2, SECTION 2

The Dedalus family begins to feel its financial troubles more acutely, and the moving men arrive to dismantle the house for a move to Dublin. In Dublin, Stephen enjoys more freedom than before, as his father is busy and Uncle Charles has grown senile. Stephen explores the city and wanders along the docks, still imagining himself as the Count of Monte Cristo. He is taken on visits to see his aunt and to see another elderly female relative.

Stephen senses in himself a new mood of bitterness, as he criticizes his own foolish impulses but finds himself unable to control them. His interactions with his aunt are awkward and result in misunderstandings. At a birthday party for another child, Stephen feels no gaiety or fun, and merely watches the other guests silently. Though he sings a song with the others, he enjoys feeling separate from the other children. However, he is attracted to one of the girls, E. C., at the party. They leave the party together and take the same tram home, riding on different levels but conversing for the entire ride. Stephen is attracted to the black stockings she wears, and recalls Eileen Vance. He wonders whether E. C. wants him to touch her and kiss her, but he does nothing.

At home, Stephen writes a love poem in his notebook, titling it "To E— C—" in imitation of Byron. He finds himself confusingly overwhelmed by a longing for romance. As summer comes to an end, Stephen is told that he will be going to a new school because his father is no longer able to afford Clongowes.

ANALYSIS: CHAPTER 2, SECTIONS 1–2

These early sections of Chapter 2 are dominated by a sense of decline, which manifests itself in several different forms. Stephen sees the reliable constancy of boyhood give way to a new sense that people and places change, and very often get worse. Uncle Charles is a sympathetic, eccentric figure in the first section of the chapter, but by the second has become senile and can no longer go out with Stephen. Similarly, Mike Flynn had once been a great runner, but now looks laughable when he runs. Most important, the Dedalus family's financial situation falls from relative prosperity to near poverty. The moving men's dismantling of the family home mirrors the dismantling of Stephen's earlier naïve faith in the world. Indeed, witnessing this slow slide into mediocrity affects Stephen deeply and directly. He is unhappy even in the company of all his relatives at

Christmastime. In part, Stephen is angry with himself, but he is also angry with his change of fortune and his own changing relationship with the world around him. Stephen still feels set apart from the world, but here we begin to see the development of his capacity for moral criticism.

While the world around him declines, Stephen's own sensitivities become more acute. In particular, we see the development of his attitude toward literature. Just as Stephen identifies with the protagonist of the children's story that his father reads to him at the beginning of the novel, he now imagines himself as the Count of Monte Cristo. These two experiences of reading show how Stephen's identification with a literary character shapes his perceptions of himself. Unlike the young boy in the children's story, Stephen's new role model, the count, is active, adventurous, heroic, and even somewhat dangerous. Like the count, who is a pursuer of vengeance and a righter of wrongs, Stephen is frustrated with the unfairness he sees in the world. In showing these relationships that Stephen forges with literary characters, Joyce implies that literature is not necessarily a solitary pursuit. Indeed, Stephen's friendship with Aubrey Mills is largely based on a shared passion for imitating Dumas's novel. Literature also helps guide Stephen's newly burgeoning sexuality, which he is able to channel into dreams of pursuing Mercédès, the heroine of *The Count of Monte Cristo*. Stephen finds romantic models in literature again when he uses a love verse by Lord Byron as a model for the poem he writes to E. C., the girl after whom he lusts at the birthday party. The intertwining of life and literature foreshadows the later ways in which the "Artist" and the "Young Man" of the title—one who creates art, and another who lives life—complement and reinforce each other.

Stephen's love interests develop in a complex manner. He experiences a tension between his somewhat awkward real-life erotic encounters and his idealized vision of gallantly pursuing Mercédès, the heroine of Dumas's novel. Yet Stephen's vision of ideal love is less a desire for a perfect love object than a hope of possessing a woman. The Count of Monte Cristo, on whom Stephen models his own idea of love, ultimately rebuffs Mercédès with the pithy rejection, "Madam, I never eat muscatel grapes." Stephen's fantasy, then, is not one of a love-filled romance, but one of repudiating a woman who desires him. The ambivalent nature of Stephen's desire manifests itself again when he stares, smitten, at a girl at a party, but then lets nothing come of it. Indeed, while he is staring, Stephen actually contemplates not the girl at the party but his first crush, Eileen Vance, whom he had watched years before. Unlike that of a traditional romantic hero, Stephen's desire for women is jumbled and confusing.

CHAPTER 2, SECTIONS 3–4

SUMMARY: CHAPTER 2, SECTION 3

Stephen, now a teenager, is a student at Belvedere College, a Jesuit school. He is preparing for a performance in the play the school is putting on for Whitsuntide, the Christian feast of Pentecost. Stephen is to play the role of a farcical teacher, a role he has won because of his height and his serious manners. After watching various others get ready for the performance, he wanders outdoors, where his school friend Vincent Heron and Heron's friend Wallis greet him. Heron encourages Stephen to imitate the school rector when performing the role of the stodgy teacher. The two boys tease Stephen for not smoking. Wallis and Heron also playfully mention that they saw Mr. Dedalus arrive at the theater with a young girl. Stephen imagines that the girl is the one Stephen had flirted with earlier at the birthday party. Wallis and Heron playfully try to force Stephen to confess his dalliance with the girl.

Stephen suddenly recalls a dispute with Heron and two other students over the question of which English poet is the best. Stephen named Byron, while the other student said that Tennyson was obviously superior. Remembering the quarrel, Stephen reflects on his father's command for him to be a good gentleman and a good Catholic, but the words sound hollow to him now. Stephen is shaken from his reverie by a reminder that the curtain will go up soon. Stephen performs his role successfully. After the play, he does not stop to talk to his father, but goes walking in the town, highly agitated.

SUMMARY: CHAPTER 2, SECTION 4

Stephen and his father sit in a railway carriage bound for the city of Cork, where his father is auctioning off some property. Stephen is bored by his father's sentimental tales of old friends and annoyed by his drinking. Falling asleep at Maryborough, Stephen is awakened by a frightening vision, in which he imagines the villagers asleep in the towns passing by outside his window. After praying, he falls asleep again to the sound of the train.

Stephen and Mr. Dedalus take a room at the Victoria Hotel. Stephen lies in bed while his father washes and grooms, softly singing a tune from a popular variety show. Stephen compliments his father on his singing. At breakfast, Stephen listens while his father questions the waiter about old acquaintances, and the waiter misunderstands which men Mr. Dedalus is discussing.

Visiting Mr. Dedalus's medical school, Stephen finds the startling word "Foetus" carved into the top of one of the desks in a lecture hall. Stephen has a vision of a mustached student carving the word years ago, to the amusement of onlookers. Leaving the college, he listens to his father's stories of the old days. Mr. Dedalus tells Stephen that he should always socialize with gentlemen. Stephen feels overwhelmed by a sense of shame and alienation, and regains his grip on himself by telling himself his own name and identity. Going from bar to bar with Mr. Dedalus, Stephen is ashamed by his father's drinking and flirtation with barmaids. They encounter an old friend of Mr. Dedalus, a little old man who jokes that he is twenty-seven years old. Stephen feels distant from his father, and recalls a poem by Shelley about the moon wandering the sky in solitude.

ANALYSIS: CHAPTER 2, SECTIONS 3–4

Stephen grows increasingly alienated from his father, largely because of Mr. Dedalus's inability to connect with reality. Stephen is bored by his father's tales of the old days as he rides with him in the train to Cork. He sees how much his father has lost touch with the world: Mr. Dedalus is unable even to talk to the hotel waiter about common acquaintances, as he and the waiter get mixed up about which acquaintance they are discussing. Mr. Dedalus's failure to keep up with the times seems pathetic, and we sense that his constant drinking throughout this nostalgic trip home is an attempt to protect himself from the pain he cannot face directly. Mr. Dedalus revisits his former medical school, perhaps to recapture his lost youth, but the visit is repulsive to Stephen, who has a vision of a student from his father's era carving the disgustingly incongruous word he sees on the table. Here again, Mr. Dedalus's blithely sweet memories of the past seem irrelevant to the family's hard times in the present, and his drunken denial of the reality around him alienates his son. When Stephen states his name for his own reassurance, saying, "I am Stephen Dedalus," we sense that he feels the need to assert his own identity because his father's identity is rapidly crumbling.

Stephen's role in the Whitsuntide play foreshadows the role of hero he later aspires to fulfill. The fact that Stephen has been chosen to play a teacher is significant, but also ironic, as the role requires that Stephen play the teacher comically rather than seriously. This parody of a teacher figure hints at the novel's underlying doubt about the validity of leading or instructing others. Stephen performs the role successfully, and is amazed at how lifelike the play feels: the "disjointed lifeless thing had suddenly assumed a life of its own. It seemed now to play itself. . . ." The life Stephen discerns in the play makes him aware of the importance of acting as a metaphor for living. Stephen's awareness of life's drama becomes problematic, however, when the things he previously thought real begin to appear false. He reflects on the moralizing voices of his early years that "had now come to be hollow-sounding in his ears." Art and life are, in a sense, switching places: while the artistic performance seems lifelike, life itself seems artificial.

Joyce's experimentation with the technique of stream of consciousness—capturing the processes and rhythms by which characters think—is especially evident in the sudden flashbacks of the play scene. Joyce narrates Heron's and Wallis's near violent teasing about Stephen's flirtation with the girl in the audience. Then suddenly, without any warning, Joyce takes us back to Stephen's first year at Belvedere, when he was accused of heresy because of a mistake he made in an essay. This memory segues into another memory from a few nights after the first, when Stephen was forced into a schoolboy argument about the relative merits of Byron and Tennyson. When this argument is finished, the narration returns to the scene of the play in the present moment. Joyce wants us to feel unsettled and even a bit confused by these unannounced leaps from present to past. The time shifts represent the way Stephen's mind—and the human mind in general—impulsively makes constant connections between experiences from the present and memories from the past. We are never told why Stephen's mind links the girl, the literary dispute, and the heresy accusation, which leaves us with an impression of psychological complexity that we cannot fully unravel.

CHAPTER 2, SECTION 5– CHAPTER 3, SECTION 1

SUMMARY: CHAPTER 2, SECTION 5

Stephen and Mr. Dedalus enter the Bank of Ireland, leaving the rest of the family waiting outside, so that Stephen can cash the check for thirty-three pounds he has received as a literary prize. Mr. Dedalus muses patriotically about the fact that the Bank of Ireland is housed in the former Irish Parliament building. Outside, the family discusses where to have dinner, and Stephen invites them to a fancy restaurant. This initiates a great spending spree in which Stephen regales his family members with costly gifts, treats, and loans.

Stephen's prize money is soon depleted, leaving him upset by his foolishness. He had hoped that spending the money would bring the family together and appease some of their animosities, but he realizes it has not worked—he feels as alienated from his family as ever. Stephen begins wandering the streets at night, tormented by sexual cravings. One night, a young prostitute dressed in pink accosts him. Stephen follows her to her room. He is reluctant to kiss her at first, but they eventually have sex. It is Stephen's first sexual experience.

SUMMARY: CHAPTER 3, SECTION 1

In December, Stephen sits in his school classroom, daydreaming about the nice stew of mutton, potatoes, and carrots he hopes to have later. He imagines that his belly is urging him to stuff himself. Stephen's thoughts soon turn to the wandering he will embark on at night and the variety of prostitutes who will proposition him. He is unable to focus on the mathematical equation in his notebook, which seems to spread out before his eyes like a peacock's tail. He contemplates the universe, and imagines he hears a distant music in it. He is aware of a "cold lucid indifference" that grips him. Hearing a fellow student answer one of the teacher's questions stupidly, Stephen feels contempt for his classmates.

On his wall, Stephen has a scroll testifying to his leadership of a society devoted to the Virgin Mary. Mary fascinates him, and with pleasure he reads a Latin passage dedicated to her, reveling in its music. At first, Stephen does not see his veneration of Mary as being at odds with his sinful habit of visiting prostitutes, but he gradually becomes more worried about his sins of the flesh. He realizes that from the sin of lust, other sins such as gluttony and greed have emerged. The school rector announces a retreat in honor of the celebration of St. Francis Xavier, whom he praises as a great soldier of God. Stephen feels his soul wither at these words.

ANALYSIS:
CHAPTER 2, SECTION 5–CHAPTER 3, SECTION 1
These sections explore the relationship between worldly pleasures and sin. The scene in which Stephen cashes his prize money is the first of several episodes in the novel that focus intensely on money and the thrill money evokes. The prize money Stephen wins seems strangely connected to his religion: the sum, thirty-three pounds, echoes Christ's age when he was crucified. Stephen confuses monetary and spiritual matters when he attempts to purchase familial harmony with money and gifts. In Christian theology, the sin of trying to exchange spiritual things for worldly ones is known as simony, a word that recalls the name of Stephen's father, Simon. This implies that such confusion of the material with the spiritual— with concepts such as faith and love—may be part of Simon's legacy to his son. Indeed, Stephen does have trouble seeing the incompatibility of some of his actions with his religious beliefs, venerating Mary even as he daydreams about visiting prostitutes. However, when Stephen says that his soul withers as he hears the rector praise St. Francis Xavier, it is clear that Stephen knows the church would view his acts as sinful.

Stephen's relationship with women becomes more complex in this section. He simultaneously displays a fervent devotion to the Virgin Mary and an obsession with visiting whores. In both cases, Stephen relates to women not as individuals but as representatives of a type. Both Mary and the prostitutes are described more as myths or dreams than as any element of everyday life. Stephen portrays Mary in a highly poetic and exotic manner, using evocative words such as "spikenard," "myrrh," and "rich garments" to describe her, and associating her with the morning star, bright and musical. However, when Stephen muses that the lips with which he reads a prayer to Mary are the same lips that have lewdly kissed a whore, we see that he has mysteriously linked the images of the whore and the Virgin in his mind as opposite visions of womanliness. Indeed, Stephen describes his encounter with the prostitute in terms similar to a prayer to Mary: when he kisses her, he "bow[s] his head" and "read[s] the meaning of her movements." When Stephen closes his eyes, "surrendering himself to her," this quiet submission mimics the Christian surrender to the Holy Spirit. Moreover, both the Virgin Mary and the prostitute represent a refuge from everyday strife, doubts, and alienation. Stephen attempts to flee mentally to the pure realm of the Virgin Mary when he is repelled by the stupidity of his classmates. Similarly, Stephen flees to the prostitute after reaching the dismal realization that his financial efforts have done nothing to allay the discord in his family. Like Mary, the prostitute offers him a chance to escape the discord around him in an almost religious way, if only momentarily.

CHAPTER 3, SECTION 2

SUMMARY

Stephen sits in the chapel as Father Arnall, appearing as a guest lecturer in Stephen's new school, reads a verse from the book of Ecclesiastes. The sight of his teacher reawakens Stephen's childhood memories of Clongowes, especially the time he was thrown into the cesspool and his subsequent recuperation in the infirmary. Father Arnall announces to the students that he is there to announce a retreat marking the day of St. Francis Xavier, patron saint of the college. The retreat, he explains, will not be simply a holiday from classes, but a withdrawal into inner contemplation of the soul, and of the soul's need to heed the four "last things": death, judgment, heaven, and hell. Father Arnall urges the boys to put aside all worldly thoughts and win the blessing of the soul's salvation.

Walking home in silence with his classmates, Stephen is aggrieved by the thought of the rich meal he has just eaten, and thinks it has made him into a bestial and greasy creature. The next day he falls even deeper into despair over the degraded state of his soul, suffering in agony and feeling a "deathchill." He imagines his weak and rotting body on its deathbed, unable to find the salvation it needs. Even worse, he pictures the Day of Judgment, when God will punish sinners with no hope of appeal or mercy.

Crossing the square, Stephen hears the laugh of a young girl. He thinks of Emma, pained by the thought that his filthy sexual escapades with prostitutes have soiled Emma's innocence. With feverish regret, he recalls all the whores with whom he has committed sins of the flesh. When this fit of shame passes, Stephen feels unable to raise his soul from its abject powerlessness. God and the

Holy Virgin seem too far from him to help, until he imagines the Virgin reaching down to join his hands with Emma's in loving union. Stephen listens to the rain falling on the chapel and imagines another biblical flood coming.

When the service resumes, Father Arnall delivers a sermon about hell, recounting the original sin of Lucifer and his fellow angels who fell from heaven at God's command. Father Arnall describes the torments of hell in terrifying detail, beginning with the physical horrors. He graphically depicts the pestilential air of the place, spoiled by the stench of rotting bodies, and the fires of hell that rage intensely and eternally. The blood and the brains of the sinner boil with no hope of relief as he lies in hell's lake of fire. Even worse, warns Father Arnall, is the horrid company that must be endured by the hell-dweller: devils as well as other sinners.

The sermon leaves Stephen paralyzed with fear, recognizing that hell is his destination. After chapel, he numbly listens to the trivial talk of the other students, who are not as affected by the sermon as he is. In English class, Stephen can think only of his soul. When a messenger arrives with news that confessions are being heard, Stephen tries to imagine himself confessing, and is terrified. Back in chapel, Father Arnall continues his tour of hell by focusing on its spiritual torments, which horrify Stephen no less than the physical ones have earlier. Together with Father Arnall, all the boys pray for God's forgiveness.

ANALYSIS

In this section, we see Joyce borrowing from classic works of literature in innovative ways. Father Arnall's vision of hell, which leads to a turning point in young Stephen's life, draws heavily from Dante Alighieri's poem *Inferno,* which tells the story of Dante's descent into hell. *Inferno* is a landmark in the genre of spiritual autobiography—the recounting of a soul's progression through righteous and sinful states. *A Portrait of the Artist as a Young Man* offers another such spiritual autobiography, as Joyce explores his own spiritual history through the character of Stephen Dedalus. Joyce places Stephen's glimpse of hell at the exact center of his novel, giving it a structure similar to that of Dante's *Divine Comedy,* of which *Inferno* is the first part. *Inferno* places the devil at the center of the Earth, so that the pilgrim seeking God must go downward before he ascends upward toward salvation. Similarly, Stephen's path has been a decline into sin and immorality that brings him to this fearful central view of hell. Just as Dante's despair is eased by the appearance of the Virgin Mary beckoning him upward to heavenly union with his beloved Beatrice, Stephen receives a vision of Mary placing his hand in his beloved Emma's. The visit to the inferno reveals unspeakable torments, but nonetheless offers a way out, a path toward ultimate holy love.

In this chapter, Stephen undergoes more than a mere vision or tour of hell—the agonies he suffers during the sermon seem closer to the experience of hell itself. He does not simply picture hell's flames in his mind's eye, but actually feels the flames on his body: "His flesh shrank together as if it felt the approach of the ravenous tongues of flames." In addition, he does not just imagine the boiling brains described by the preacher, but actually senses that "[h]is brain was simmering and bubbling within the cracking tenement of the skull." Stephen's close identification with the subject of the sermon sets him apart from his fellow students, who later chat casually about it. This dissimilar reaction reiterates the fact that Stephen is a social outsider. He experiences spiritual yearnings more immediately and intensely than others, even feeling them physically.

Stephen's experience as he contemplates the religious sermon binds his perceptions of past and future. Stephen's horror of hell is largely a horror of sufferings to come in the future, which he experiences as if they are in the present. He lives through his own future death: "He, he himself, his body to which he had yielded was dying. Into the grave with it! Nail it down into a wooden box, the corpse." Stephen's imagination carries him still farther into the future, all the way to the equally terrifying Judgment Day. However, while religion forces Stephen to face the future, it also forces him to confront the past. Father Arnall visits the school like a figure out of Stephen's memory, a ghost from years gone by. Stephen responds to the visit with a return to infancy: "His soul, as these memories came back to him, became again a child's soul." Stephen's encounter with the past is more than just memory—it is a momentary change in his very soul. Thus, Arnall's sermon prompts Stephen both back toward childhood and forward toward death, reaching out to both extremes of his life. The novel suggests that the aims of autobiography and the aims of religion are similar, as both lead individuals to integrate their present, past, and future lives in an attempt to make sense of the whole.

SUMMARY & ANALYSIS

CHAPTER 3, SECTION 3–
CHAPTER 4, SECTION 1

SUMMARY: CHAPTER 3, SECTION 3

Another life! A life of grace and virtue and happiness!
It was true. It was not a dream from which he would
wake. The past was past. (See QUOTATIONS, p. 50)

Stephen goes up to his room after dinner in order to "be alone with his soul." He feels fear and despair as he pauses at the threshold, worrying that evil creatures are in the room waiting for him. Going in, he is relieved to find that it is just his ordinary room. Stephen feels weak and numb. He admits to himself the horror of all the sins he has committed, and is amazed that God has not stricken him dead yet. Lying down, Stephen closes his eyes and has a fearful vision of a field covered in weeds and excrement, occupied by six ghoulish goatlike creatures with gray skin. Swishing their tails menacingly, the creatures trace ever-smaller circles around Stephen, uttering incomprehensible words.

Springing awake from this nightmare, Stephen rushes frantically to open the window for some fresh air. He finds that the rain has stopped and the skies are full of promise. He prays to Jesus, weeping for his lost innocence. Walking through the streets that evening, Stephen knows he must confess. He asks an old woman where the nearest chapel is, and goes to it immediately. He anxiously waits for his turn to enter the confessional. When it is finally Stephen's turn, the priest asks how long it has been since his last confession, and Stephen replies that it has been eight months. He confesses that he has had sexual relations with a woman and that he is only sixteen. The priest offers forgiveness and Stephen heads home feeling filled with grace. He goes to sleep. The next day he finds himself at the altar with his classmates and receives the Sacrament.

SUMMARY: CHAPTER 4, SECTION 1

Stephen imposes a new system of religious discipline upon himself that transforms his life. He prays every morning before a holy image, yet his sense of triumph is lessened by his uncertainty whether his prayers are sufficient to counteract the ill effects of all his sins. He divides his daily schedule into parts that correspond to particular spiritual functions. Stephen keeps rosary beads in his trouser pockets so that he can touch them as he walks, and he divides each rosary into three parts devoted to the three theological virtues. Reading books of devotional literature, Stephen learns about the three aspects of the Holy Trinity. Though he cannot understand the solemn mystery of the Trinity, he finds the mystery easier to accept than God's love for his soul.

Gradually, however, Stephen comes to accept the fact that God loves him, and he begins to see the whole world as one vast expression of divine love. He is careful not to get carried away by his spiritual triumphs, and he pursues even the lowliest devotion carefully. Stephen avoids making eye contact with women, and sniffs the most objectionable odors he can find, in order to "mortify" his sense of smell. He never consciously changes positions in bed. Despite his attempts at self-discipline, he is periodically tempted by sin and bothered by sudden fits of impatience, as when his mother sneezes. Stephen comforts himself, however, with the knowledge that strong temptations prove that his fortress is holding tight against the devil's attacks. He asks himself whether he has corrected his life.

ANALYSIS:
CHAPTER 3, SECTION 3–CHAPTER 4, SECTION 1
Stephen begins fervently to apply spiritual discipline to his own actions, in contrast to his passive status as a member of the audience listening to Father Arnall's sermon and attempting to understand it academically. Long passages during the sermon make no mention of Stephen at all, as the focus is on hell itself. Here, however, we focus on Stephen's reaction, which is no longer passive. His withdrawal into himself is not only described in psychological terms, but in physical ones as well, as when he goes to his room "to be alone with his soul." In applying the knowledge from the sermon, Stephen becomes the master of his spiritual fate. Even his dream of hell indicates a more active relationship with the torments he undergoes, as the goat-like devils come from his own mind as his own creations. Since they are products of Stephen's own mind, he can disregard them if he wishes. Therefore, as scary as the goat nightmare is, it is something of a release and a relief for Stephen, who runs to the window to be soothed by the fresh air. His decision to confess his sins is the next step in his gradual process of taking control of his spiritual state.

Stephen's rigorous program of spiritual self-discipline is impressive, and demonstrates his extraordinary earnestness. The unbelievable asceticism that he willingly adopts demonstrates his strength of will and suggests his heroism. Like some of the early ascetics and hermits of the Christian Church, who lived in the desert and ate locusts, Stephen displays an astonishing ability to overcome his bodily longings and to affirm the superiority of the soul. In doing so, he proves his similarity to martyrs and saints.

However, Joyce suggests that a saint's life may not be desirable for Stephen. Joyce's style, which is richly detailed and concretely sensual in earlier sections of the novel, now becomes extremely dry, abstract, and academic. This style corresponds with Stephen's psychological state: as Stephen becomes more ascetic and self-depriving, Joyce's language loses its colorful adjectives and complex syntax. The very difficulty of reading such dry language suggests the difficulty of the life that Stephen is leading. Stephen's question at the end of Chapter 4, Section 1—"I have amended my life, have I not?"—emphasizes the fact that Joyce himself has amended his prose. Importantly, though Stephen explicitly acknowledges that his life has been changed, he does not say that it has necessarily improved. His heroic efforts to deprive himself are impressive, but do not necessarily make him a better person.

CHAPTER 4, SECTIONS 2–3

This was the call of life to his soul not the dull gross voice of the world of duties and despair, not the inhuman voice that had called him to the pale service of the altar. (See QUOTATIONS, p. 51)

SUMMARY: CHAPTER 4, SECTION 2

Vacation has ended and Stephen is back in his Jesuit school, where he has been mysteriously summoned to a meeting with the director. Stephen goes to the director and listens to his idle discussion about whether or not the Capuchin priestly robe should be eliminated. The director laughingly refers to the robe as a "jupe," meaning "skirt" in French. Stephen feels awkward. The "jupe" reference calls up thoughts of women's undergarments in Stephen's mind. Stephen wonders why the director makes mention of skirts, and it occurs to him that the priest may be testing Stephen's response to the mention of women. The director asks Stephen whether he has ever felt he has a vocation, and urges him to consider a life in the church. The director says that the priesthood is the greatest honor bestowed on a man, but adds that it is a very serious decision to make.

At first, Stephen is intrigued by the thought of the priesthood, and pictures himself in the admired, respected role of the silent and serious priest carrying out his duties. As he imagines the bland and ordered life awaiting him in the church, however, he begins to feel a deep unrest burning inside him. He walks back home from school and passes a shrine to the Virgin Mary, but feels surprisingly cold toward it.

When Stephen sees his disorderly house, he knows that his fate is to learn wisdom not in the refuge of the church, but "among the snares of the world." Arriving home, he asks his brothers and sisters where their parents are. He learns that his parents are looking for yet another house because the family is about to be thrown out of its current one. Stephen reflects on how weary his siblings seem even before they have started on life's journey.

SUMMARY: CHAPTER 4, SECTION 3

Stephen impatiently waits for his father and tutor to return with news about the possibility of his admission into the university. Stephen's mother is hostile to the idea, but Stephen feels that a great fate is in store for him. He sets off walking toward the sea, encountering a group of teacher friars on the way. He considers greeting them, but concludes that it is impossible to imagine them being generous toward him. He recites snatches of poetry and regards the light on the water. Stephen comes upon several of his schoolmates who are swimming, and they jokingly greet him as they say his name in Greek.

Reflecting on the myth of Daedalus that his name evokes, Stephen ponders his similarity to that "fabulous artificer" who constructed wings with which he flew out of imprisonment. Stephen is suddenly enraptured by this thought, and feels that he will soon begin building a new soul that will allow him to rise above current miseries. At that moment, he sees a beautiful girl wading in the water, her skirts hiked up high. He and the girl make eye contact for a moment. Stephen perceives her as an angel of youth and beauty, and he swoons inwardly. In the evening, he climbs a hill and watches the moon.

ANALYSIS: CHAPTER 4, SECTIONS 2–3

Although Stephen's path through life continues to be guided by females, the kinds of women who influence him change as he grows older. The Virgin Mary has been Stephen's main object of devotion, but now she seems to have lost her power over him. When he passes by a shrine to the Virgin on his way home from school, he glances at it "coldly," no longer stirred by her presence. The school director's odd emphasis on the word "jupe," meaning "skirt," implies that some other woman may have replaced Mary in Stephen's heart. Stephen's turn away from the church and toward the world is emphasized when he turns from the Virgin to the beautiful girl he sees bathing. Importantly, this shift occurs directly after Stephen contemplates Daedalus's use of art to achieve freedom—a suggestion that Stephen will do the same. The bathing girl is a secular version of the Virgin Mary, an emblem of a means to rise to heaven, but without the church.

Joyce's novels are notable for their allusions to classic works of literature, as seemingly insignificant comments or phrases are often references to other novels, plays, or poems. One of the primary sources on which Joyce draws in *A Portrait of the Artist as a Young Man* is Greek myth. The mythic aspect of the novel emerges clearly in this section with the reference to Daedalus. In Greek mythology, Daedalus was a renowned craftsman who built a pair of wings for himself and a pair for his son, in an attempt to escape imprisonment on the island of Crete. In this novel, Stephen's view of himself changes when his friends address him with a Greek version of his name. He suddenly begins to reflect on certain affinities between himself and that mythical "fabulous artificer," no longer defining himself through Christian doctrine by relating himself to Christ and Mary. Rather, Stephen turns to pagan sources and inspirations in his quest for self-definition. His name is significant. His first name alludes to the first Christian martyr, St. Stephen. His surname, however, alludes to a pagan character whose skill allows him to rise high above the world. In this section, Stephen begins to shift his emphasis from his first name to his last name. He dwells on the idea of Daedalus's flight-giving wings, a piece of artisan handicraft that symbolizes the individual's ability to create art and the possibility of transcending worldly woes. Much as Daedalus escaped prison, Stephen dreams of escaping the misery of his impoverished family and narrow, sad life.

To Stephen, the vision of his mythical namesake is not just a hint of his own fate, but a prophecy of it, a prediction that cannot be avoided. Stephen's mental image of "a hawklike man flying sunward above the sea" strikes him as a "prophecy of the end he had been born to serve and had been following through the mists of childhood and boyhood." Daedalus is a "symbol of the artist forging anew in his workshop out of the sluggish matter of the earth a new soaring impalpable imperishable being." This vision is not simply an image of his future, but of his childhood and boyhood as well. His vision reveals a hidden thread that connects Stephen's past, present, and future into one whole. Most important, perhaps, Stephen realizes that the art that he will forge is not merely a beautiful object, but an entire eternal existence. Through his art, Stephen creates an "imperishable being" very much like a soul—he will not just create literature, but will create himself.

CHAPTER 5, SECTIONS 1–2

—The language in which we are speaking is his before it is mine. How different are the words home, Christ, ale, master, on his lips and on mine!

(See QUOTATIONS, p. 52)

SUMMARY: CHAPTER 5, SECTION 1

Stephen eats a poor meal and examines the pawnshop tickets upon which his increasingly impoverished family survives. Mrs. Dedalus expresses her worry that Stephen's character has been changed by university life. From upstairs, Mr. Dedalus snaps that his son is a "lazy bitch." Annoyed and frustrated, Stephen leaves the house and wanders through the rainy Dublin landscape, quoting poems to himself and musing on the aesthetic theories of Aristotle and Aquinas. A nearby clock tolls eleven, reminding him of his friend MacCann. Stephen reflects on MacCann's accusation that Stephen is too socially disengaged. Stephen realizes that he is missing his English lecture, but is not overly concerned; he imagines the students meekly taking notes. On the whole, he is disappointed by university education.

As he walks to the campus, Stephen recollects a visit to his friend Davin, a handsome and athletic boy devoted to the Irish cause. Davin had told Stephen a story about being invited to spend the night with a housewife he did not know. Stephen notes that it is now too late to go to his French class and decides to head for the physics lecture hall, where he runs into the dean of studies. The dean is trying to start a fire, and the two discuss the art of igniting flames. Stephen and the dean speak about aesthetics, but Stephen is disappointed by the older man's spotty knowledge, and the conversation is awkward. When Stephen uses the word "tundish," referring to a funnel for adding oil to a lamp, the dean does not know the word, which Stephen concludes must be Irish. Stephen reflects that English will always be a borrowed language for him, "acquired speech."

Stephen then attends a physics class that is comic and ineffectual. Afterward, Stephen chats with Cranly, MacCann, and other classmates, joking with them in Latin. MacCann urges Stephen to sign a petition for universal peace. When Stephen seems reluctant, MacCann accuses him of being an antisocial minor poet. Temple, a classmate who idolizes Stephen for his independent spirit, defends Stephen. Another student, Lynch, greets them. Davin proudly asserts his own Irish nationalist fervor, and asks Stephen why he has dropped out of Irish language class. Davin says that Stephen is a true Irishman in his heart, but too proud.

Stephen explains that the soul takes time to be born, longer than the body. Stephen explains his aesthetic theory of the ideal stasis or immobility evoked by a work of art, a theory he derives from Aristotle and Aquinas. He also explains the ideals—integrity, consonance, and radiance—that he believes every artistic object must achieve. Stephen's concept of divinity lies in the aesthetic—his God has withdrawn from the world of men, "paring his fingernails" in solitude. Stephen's point is that truly transcendent art must be above the common fray of mankind. Lynch whispers to Stephen that Stephen's beloved, an unnamed girl, is present. Stephen wonders whether he has judged this girl too harshly, and muses upon her.

SUMMARY: CHAPTER 5, SECTION 2

Stephen awakens in the morning in a mood of contentment and enchantment, having dreamed of erotic union with his beloved. Savoring the feeling, he undertakes to write down a romantic poem he has composed. He recollects being together with the girl in a room with a piano, singing and dancing, and remembers her telling him that she feels he is not a monk, but a heretic.

Stephen is jerked out of his reverie by jealous suspicions about Father Moran's interest in the girl, Emma. Stephen reflects that the last time he wrote verses to Emma was ten years ago, after they rode home together on the same tram after a birthday party. He accuses himself of folly, and wonders whether Emma has been aware of his devotion to her. Stephen feels desire flow through his body, and turns again to the villanelle, the poem he is composing.

ANALYSIS: CHAPTER 5, SECTIONS 1–2

The dean's inability to understand Stephen's use of the word "tundish" may seem like a minor detail, but it actually symbolizes the clash of cultures that is at the heart of the Irish experience. The dean is English, and represents to Stephen all the institutional power and prestige England has wielded throughout its colonial occupation of Ireland. The dean is thus a representative of cultural domination. By failing to understand Stephen's word—which is derived from Irish rather than English—the dean reminds us of the linguistic and cultural divide between England and Ireland. With sadness and despair, Stephen reflects that this divide may be unbridgeable, and his disappointment underscores the discontent he already feels for stale university life. The episode with the dean shows Stephen the importance of creating his own language, as the English he has been using is not really his own. He realizes that English "will always be for me an acquired speech. I have not made or accepted its words. My voice holds them at bay."

Joyce reinforces this idea of speaking someone else's language throughout the novel through repeated uses of quoted speech from a variety of external sources. The opening lines of the novel, for instance, are a child's story told by someone else. Later, we find Stephen frequently quoting Aquinas and Aristotle. Yet despite these constant citations, no quotation marks are used in the novel, sometimes making it difficult to tell the difference between a character borrowing someone else's words and a character speaking in his or her own voice. The "tundish" episode with the dean shows Stephen the necessity of making this distinction and the importance of creating a distinctive and truly Irish voice for himself.

Joyce also uses these sections to explore the contrast between individuality and community. Stephen is now more of a free-floating individual than ever before. His links with his family, whose sinking poverty level and carelessness repel him, are weaker than ever. His mother is disappointed with the changes university life has brought about in her son, and his father calls him a "lazy bitch." There seems to be little parental pride or affection to offset Mr. Dedalus's hostility. Moreover, Stephen's social life is hardly any less solitary. He fails to share the ideological position of any of his friends: he cannot adopt the Irish patriotism of Davin or the international pacifism of MacCann. Even the flattering adulation of Temple fails to inspire Stephen. Therefore, having given up hope on family, church, friends, and education, Stephen seems to be more alone than ever. This assessment is only partly true, however, as Stephen is never completely isolated in the novel. His family repels him, but he continues to see them and speak to them, and his warm address to his siblings shows that he still has family ties. Furthermore, even when composing epitaphs to dead friendships, Stephen is surrounded by his friends and interacts with them in a lively and outgoing way. The proximity of such human relationships is clearly important, as Stephen retains a powerful commitment to his society until the very end of the novel, even when dreaming of fashioning a new soul for himself.

CHAPTER 5, SECTIONS 3–4

SUMMARY: CHAPTER 5, SECTION 3

> Old father, old artificer, stand me now and ever in
> good stead.   (See QUOTATIONS, p. 53)

Sitting on the steps of the university library, Stephen watches a flock of birds circling above and tries to identify their species. He muses on the idea of flight and on the fact that men have always tried to fly. His thoughts turn to lines from a Yeats play that has recently opened, lines that characterize swallows as symbols of freedom. He remembers having heard harsh criticism of the play, as some young men accused Yeats of libel and atheism. Leaving the library, Stephen walks with Cranly and Temple, who fall into an argument. Stephen's beloved Emma leaves the library and nods a greeting to Cranly, ignoring Stephen. Stephen feels hurt and jealous, and envisions Emma walking home. A squat young man named Glynn approaches Stephen and his friends, and Temple engages them in a religious dispute about the fate of unbaptized children.

Leaving the rest of the students, Cranly and Stephen walk on alone. Stephen tells Cranly about an unpleasant conversation he has had at home. Stephen's mother wants him to attend Easter services in the church, but Stephen no longer feels religious faith and does not want to go. Cranly answers that a mother's love is more important than religious doubts, and advises Stephen to go. Cranly gently tests Stephen's new faithlessness by insulting Jesus and closely watching his friend's reaction. Cranly concludes that Stephen may still have vestiges of faith. Stephen sadly tells his friend that he feels he may soon have to leave the university and abandon his friends in order to pursue his artistic ambitions. Stephen says that he feels he must obey the dictum "I will not serve," refusing any ideology that is imposed upon him from above, even that of friends and family. Cranly warns Stephen of the risk of extreme solitude, but Stephen does not reply.

SUMMARY: CHAPTER 5, SECTION 4

At this point, the narrative switches to a journal form, composed of dated entries written by Stephen himself, from a first-person perspective. Stephen records his scattered impressions of thoughts, perceptions, and events of each day. He tells of his conversation with Cranly about leaving the university, and mentions Cranly's father. He distractedly muses on the fact that John the Baptist lived on locusts in the desert, and comments on his friend Lynch's pursuit of a hospital nurse. Stephen notes a conversation with his mother regarding the Virgin Mary, in which his mother accuses Stephen of reading too much and losing his faith. Stephen, however, says that he cannot repent.

Stephen speaks of a squabble with a fellow student and of attempting to read three reviews in the library. He records two dreams: one of viewing a long gallery filled with images of fabulous kings, and another of meeting strange mute creatures with phosphorescent faces. He mentions meeting his father, who asks him why he does not join a rowing club. In his entry dated April 15, Stephen records meeting "her"—meaning Emma—on Grafton Street. Emma asks Stephen whether he is writing poems and why he no longer comes to the university. Stephen excitedly talks to her about his artistic plans. The following day, he has a vision of disembodied arms and voices that seem to call to him, urging him to join them. Stephen ends his journal with a prayer to his old father, Daedalus, whom he calls "old artificer," to stand him in good stead.

ANALYSIS: CHAPTER 5, SECTIONS 3–4

Stephen's long meditation on the birds circling overhead is an important sign of his own imminent flight. He cannot identify what species the birds are, just as he is not sure about his own nature. All he knows is that the birds are flying, as he too will fly. He will build his wings alone, just as his mythical namesake Daedalus alone crafted the wings with which he escaped from his prison. The birds offer Stephen relief from his daily worries: although their cries are harsh, the "inhuman clamour soothed his ears in which his mother's sobs and reproaches murmured insistently." The significance of the birds is, however, morally ambiguous. Stephen is not sure whether the birds are "an augury of good or evil," just as he cannot be entirely sure whether his decision to leave his family, friends, and university will have good or bad consequences. Finally, the birds are a symbol of literature and national politics as well. They remind Stephen of a passage from a recent Yeats play he has just seen, lines that refer to the swallow that wanders over the waters. As the nationalist play has attracted patriotic criticism, this swallow is a potent political symbol to which Stephen responds deeply.

Joyce's transition to journal entries at the end of the novel is a formal change that highlights Stephen's continuing search for his own voice. The journal entry form explores the problem of representing a person through words. Stephen is no longer being talked about by an external narrator, but is now speaking in his own voice. This form also frames the final section of the novel with the first, which opens with a different external voice—Mr. Dedalus telling his son a story. Throughout the novel, Stephen has continued his search for a voice, first drawing on others' voices—citing Aquinas and Aristotle as authorities and quoting English poems—and later realizing that he must devise a language of his own because he cannot be happy speaking the language of others. This last section of the novel finally offers a glimpse of Stephen succeeding in doing precisely that. We finally see him imitating no one and quoting no one, offering his own perceptions, dreams, insights, and reflections through his words alone. Stylistically, this section is not as polished and structured as the earlier portions of the novel, but this lack of polish indicates its immediacy and sincerity in Stephen's mind.

Stephen's ideas of femininity become more complex in the final sections of Chapter 5, when he finally confronts Emma and talks to her on Grafton Street. Stephen's relation to females throughout the novel has been largely conflicted and abstract up to this point. This meeting with Emma, however, is concrete, placing Stephen himself in control. The conversation with Emma emphasizes the fact that women are no longer guiding Stephen: his mother no longer pushes him, the Virgin Mary no longer shows him the way, and prostitutes no longer seduce him. Women are no longer in a superior or transcendent position in his life. Finally, in actually speaking with Emma face-to-face, Stephen shows that he has begun to conceive of women as fellow human beings rather than idealized creatures. He no longer needs to be mothered and guided, as his emotional, spiritual, and artistic development has given him the vision and confidence to show himself the way.

IMPORTANT QUOTATIONS EXPLAINED

1. Once upon a time and a very good time it was there
   was a moocow coming down along the road and this
   moocow that was coming down along the road met a
   nicens little boy named baby tuckoo. . . . His father
   told him that story: his father looked at him through a
   glass: he had a hairy face. He was a baby tuckoo. The
   moocow came down the road where Betty Byrne lived:
   she sold lemon platt.
   O, the wild rose blossoms On the little green place.
   He sang that song. That was his song.
   O, the green wothe botheth.
   When you wet the bed first it is warm then it gets
   cold. His mother put on the oilsheet. That had the
   queer smell.

These first lines of *A Portrait of the Artist as a Young Man* represent Joyce's attempt to capture the perceptions of a very young boy.
The language is childish: "moocow," "tuckoo," and "nicens" are
words a child might say, or words that an adult might say to a child.
In addition to using childlike speech, Joyce tries to emulate a child's
thought processes through the syntax of his sentences and paragraphs. He jumps from thought to thought with no apparent moti-
vation or sense of time. We have no idea how much time goes by
between Stephen's father telling him the story and Stephen wetting
the bed. Moreover, the way Stephen's thoughts turn inward reflects
the way children see themselves as the center of the universe.
Stephen is the same Baby Tuckoo as the one in the story his father
tells, and the song Stephen hears is "his song." As Stephen ages,
Joyce's style becomes less childish, tracking and emulating the
thoughts and feelings of the maturing Stephen as closely as possible.

2. —*Corpus Domini nostri.* Could it be? He knelt there
sinless and timid: and he would hold upon his tongue
the host and God would enter his purified body.—*In
vitam eternam. Amen.* Another life! A life of grace
and virtue and happiness! It was true. It was not a
dream from which he would wake. The past was
past.—*Corpus Domini nostri.* The ciborium had come
to him.

One technique Joyce uses to indicate the development of Stephen's
consciousness is to end each of the five chapters with a moment of
epiphany in which Stephen recognizes the fallacy of one way of life
and the truth of another. This passage is the epiphany that ends
Chapter 3, the moment in which Stephen understands that he must
turn to a religious life. The passage demonstrates one of the most
revolutionary aspects of Joyce's narrative style: whereas other confessional novels usually involve narrators looking back at the events
of their youth with an adult perspective, *A Portrait of the Artist as a
Young Man* is not mediated by such a detached voice. When Stephen
declares, "Another life!" and "The past was past," we are given no
indication that Stephen's religious life is eventually replaced by a
calling to an artistic life. Rather, just like Stephen, we are led to
believe that he will remain religious for the rest of his life and that
the arrival of the ciborium, the container holding the host, symbolizes the arrival of his true calling. In this sense, we experience the
successive epiphanies in Stephen's life just as he experiences them,
knowing that a change is being made to life as he has lived it up to
this point, but not knowing where this change will take him in the
future.

QUOTATIONS

3.   His throat ached with a desire to cry aloud, the cry of
     a hawk or eagle on high, to cry piercingly of his
     deliverance to the winds. This was the call of life to his
     soul not the dull gross voice of the world of duties and
     despair, not the inhuman voice that had called him to
     the pale service of the altar. An instant of wild flight
     had delivered him and the cry of triumph which his
     lips withheld cleft his brain.

This passage, from Chapter 4, demonstrates Joyce's contention that becoming a true artist involves a calling, not a conscious decision the artist can make himself. These thoughts fly through Stephen's mind just before he sees a young girl wading at a beach. The sight of her image leads to one of the most important epiphanies in the novel. Stephen sees her not long after he has refused the priesthood, a time when he is unsure of what to do now that he has relinquished his religious devotion. At this moment, Stephen finally feels a strong calling, and determines to celebrate life, humanity, and freedom, ignoring all temptations to turn away from such a celebration. He has already succumbed to temptation twice: first, a "dull gross voice" causes him to sin deeply when he succumbs to the squalor of Dublin and its prostitutes; second, an "inhuman voice" invites him into the cold, dull, unfeeling world of the priesthood. Both of these temptations, as well as the calling to become an artist, are forces through which the outside world acts upon Stephen. In this context, the passage suggests that it is as much fate as Stephen's own free will that leads him to become an artist.

4.   —The language in which we are speaking is his before
it is mine. How different are the words *home, Christ,
ale, master,* on his lips and on mine! I cannot speak or
write these words without unrest of spirit. His
language, so familiar and so foreign, will always be
for me an acquired speech. I have not made or
accepted its words. My voice holds them at bay. My
soul frets in the shadow of his language.

This quotation, from Chapter 5, indicates the linguistic and historical context of *A Portrait of the Artist as a Young Man.* Stephen makes this comment during his conversation with the dean of studies. The dean, who is English, does not know what "tundish" means, and assumes it is an Irish word. In a moment of patriotism, Stephen sympathizes with the Irish people, whose very language is borrowed from their English conquerors. The words Stephen chooses as examples in this passage are significant. "Ale" and "home" show how a borrowed language can suddenly make even the most familiar things feel foreign. "Christ" alludes to the fact that even the Irish religion has been altered by English occupation. Finally, "master" refers to the subordination of the Irish to the English. Stephen's new awareness of the borrowed nature of his language has a strong effect on him, as he knows that language is central to his artistic mission. By the end of the novel, Stephen acknowledges that Irish English is a borrowed language, and resolves to use that knowledge to shape English into a tool for expressing the soul of the imprisoned Irish race.

5. *26 April:* I go to encounter for the millionth time the reality of experience and to forge in the smithy of my soul the uncreated conscience of my race.

    27 April: Old father, old artificer, stand me now and ever in good stead.

These final lines of the novel proclaim Stephen's aim to be an artist for the rest of his life. The phrase "the smithy of my soul" indicates that he strives to be an artist whose individual consciousness is the foundation for all of his work. The reference to "the uncreated conscience of my race" implies that he strives to be an artist who uses his individual voice to create a voice and conscience for the community into which he has been born. The final diary entry, with its references to "old father" and "old artificer," reinforces Stephen's twofold mission. He invokes his "old father"—which can be read as either Simon Dedalus or Ireland itself—to acknowledge his debt to his past. He invokes the "old artificer"—his namesake, Daedalus, the master craftsman from ancient mythology—to emphasize his role as an artist. It is through his art that Stephen will use his individuality to create a conscience for his community.

Key Facts

FULL TITLE
A Portrait of the Artist as a Young Man

AUTHOR
James Joyce

TYPE OF WORK
Novel

GENRE
Bildungsroman, autobiographical novel

LANGUAGE
English

TIME AND PLACE WRITTEN
1907–1915; Trieste, Dublin, Zurich

DATE OF FIRST PUBLICATION
1916

PUBLISHER
B. W. Huebsch, New York

NARRATOR
The narrator is anonymous, and speaks with the same voice and tone that Stephen might

POINT OF VIEW
Although most of *A Portrait of the Artist as a Young Man* is in the third person, the point of view is Stephen's: as Stephen develops as a person, the language and perspective of the narration develop with him. We see everything in the manner in which he thinks and feels it. At the very end of the novel, there is a brief section in which the story is told through Stephen's diary entries. This section is in the first person.

TONE
The tone is generally serious and introspective, especially during Stephen's several heartfelt epiphanies

TENSE
Past

SETTING (TIME)
1882–1903

SETTING (PLACE)
Primarily Dublin and the surrounding area

PROTAGONIST
Stephen Dedalus

MAJOR CONFLICT
Stephen struggles to decide whether he should be loyal to his
family, his church, his nation, or his vocation as an artist

RISING ACTION
Stephen's encounters with prostitutes; his emotional reaction to
Father Arnall's hellfire sermons; his temporary devotion to
religious life; his realization that he must confront the decision
of whether to center his life around religion or art

CLIMAX
Stephen's decision in Chapter 4 to reject the religious life in
favor of the life of an artist

FALLING ACTION
Stephen's enrollment in University College, where he gradually
forms his aesthetic theory; Stephen's distancing of himself from
his family, church, and nation

THEMES
Development of individual consciousness; the pitfalls of
religious extremism; the role of the artist; the need for
Irish autonomy

MOTIFS
Music; flight; prayers, secular songs, and Latin phrases

SYMBOLS
Green and maroon; Emma; the girl on the beach

FORESHADOWING
Stephen's heartfelt emotional and aesthetic experiences
foreshadow his ultimate acceptance of the life of an artist.
Additionally, Joyce often refers to Stephen's vague sense, even
very early in his life, that a great destiny awaits him.

Study Questions & Essay Topics

Study Questions

1. *How is Stephen influenced by his Irish nationality?*

Stephen has a conflicted relationship to his Irish nationality, largely because of the fact that his family and friends have conflicting political views about Ireland and its independence. On one hand, Stephen's governess, Dante, is proud of the church and disdainful of Irish leaders like Parnell. On the other hand, Mr. Dedalus and John Casey see Parnell as the only hope for a free Ireland. Stephen's friends also stand on opposing sides of the question. Influenced by these divergent opinions, Stephen, though eager to leave Ireland by the end of the novel, is also inextricably tied to it. He feels that Ireland has always been at the mercy of other nations, just as he has always been bound by outside influences. When Stephen leaves, it is to forge the conscience of the Irish race—a project that, ironically, he feels he can accomplish only by leaving his native island behind.

2. *Discuss Joyce's use of religious imagery and language.
    Why are Father Arnall's three sermons so successful in
    overcoming Stephen's religious doubt?*

Father Arnall's sermons touch Stephen at his core because they res-
onate with both Stephen's cultural background and his preoccupa-
tion with aesthetics. At the time when Father Arnall delivers his
sermons, Stephen is struggling with the exact issues the priest
addresses: the overwhelming strength of sinful emotions and the
fear of being punished for them. When Father Arnall speaks, he val-
idates and solidifies Stephen's vague concerns about morality and
punishment in the afterlife. The cultural context in which Stephen
has been raised creates an intolerable tension between his desire for
various freedoms and his desire to meet the moral requirements
placed upon him.

Additionally, Stephen, who is closely attentive to the sensory
world around him, particularly connects with Father Arnall's vivid
portraits of the sensory experience of being in hell. In addition to
focusing on spiritual tortures, the priest describes the raw pain and
grotesqueness of hell, painting a moral and religious punishment in
emotional and aesthetic terms. As Stephen is just awakening to the
power of such emotions and aesthetics, Father Arnall's sermons
have a particular resonance for him. Stephen's conversion to devout
religiousness is, however, only temporary. The same tools Father
Arnall uses to such great effect in his sermons soon convert Stephen
from a would-be priest of religion to a confirmed priest of art.

3. *What role does Stephen's burgeoning sexuality play in his development as a character? How does his Catholic morality complicate his experience of sexuality?*

Stephen's early life is dominated by moral restrictions embedded in the society and family surrounding him, and his coming-of-age process involves confronting and dismantling these restrictions. Stephen grows up enthralled by the hierarchies and rituals of school and church, a structure in which his growing adolescent lust is not acknowledged or validated. His newfound sexuality is so alien, in fact, that he initially fails to recognize it, and it is not until he falls into the arms of the prostitute that he realizes what he has been longing for. The encounter with the prostitute awakens Stephen to a side of his character that has until then been hidden. The encounter symbolizes not only his awakening sexuality, but more generally, his awakening to the power of emotion and art. It also illustrates his extremely polarized conception of women: on the one hand are prostitutes with whom he can express his feelings of sexual desire, and on the other are revered, distant, near saintly figures such as Emma, whom he loves from afar but can never approach.

4.   *Compare and contrast Stephen's perception of art with his*
     perception of religion, family, school, or country. What
     makes art such an appealing escape for Stephen?

For Stephen, art offers an escape from the constraints of religion,
family, school, and country. Constrained by his surroundings and
even his own self-imposed restraints, he looks to art as an independent, abstract realm where he can create a world that suits him.
Stephen's obsession with aesthetic theory indicates that, for him, art
is an abstract idea. Unlike the abstractions of religion, however, the
abstractions of art are tied to the emotions with which Stephen
struggles. In his love poem "To E— C—," for instance, he finds an
outlet both for his aesthetic leanings and for the emotions that he is
too restrained—or afraid—to express.

5.   *Why does Stephen turn down the offer to become a Jesuit?*

Religion is Stephen's life up until the point when he is offered the possibility of entering the Jesuit order. After confessing his sins, he has tried to purify himself, and his superiors notice this remarkable devotion. It would seem that an offer to join the Jesuits is the perfect culmination of a life that, aside from occasional lapses such as liaisons with prostitutes, has been destined for religion. Stephen, however, rejects the Jesuit offer as soon as it is made. Joyce suggests that Stephen clings to religion not because it is his calling, but merely as a source of stability within his turbulent life. He uses religion in an attempt to erect a barrier against the emotions that rage within him. Furthermore, Stephen has a strong aesthetic objection to the idea of being a priest, an objection that is emphasized by the washed-out character of the priest who offers him the position. Even if the religious life appeals to Stephen on a religious or abstract level, the idea of walking, dressing, talking, and living like a priest is aesthetically unpleasant. At this point in the novel, Stephen's aesthetic inclinations have become so strong that he almost inevitably rejects anything that contradicts these aesthetic values.

SUGGESTED ESSAY TOPICS

1. How do Stephen's parents affect his development throughout the novel? How does he react to his father's patriotic nostalgia? To his mother's solemn Catholicism? At the end of the novel, why does Stephen feel he needs to escape from his family?

2. The passages at the very beginning of the novel recreate Stephen's early childhood in a sequence of memories and perceptions. Are these passages effective in recreating the thoughts and feelings of a very young boy? Why or why not?

3. How does Stephen's aesthetic theory relate to the doctrine of Christianity or the behavior of hedonism?

4. Compare and contrast Stephen with some of the other boys and young men with whom he associates. How is he different from them? How does he feel about being different?

5. How does the setting of the novel affect the characters and the plot?

REVIEW & RESOURCES

QUIZ

1. What does Stephen's father call him as a child?

   A. Baby tuckoo
   B. Baby butter
   C. Moocow
   D. Lemon platt

2. Where does Stephen attend school as a child?

   A. Trinity
   B. Clongowes
   C. Athy
   D. Eton

3. Why do John Casey and Dante argue at Stephen's first Christmas dinner at the adult table?

   A. Casey supports the Catholic Church and Dante is against it
   B. Casey supports Parnell and Dante is against him
   C. Casey is in favor of Stephen attending Clongowes and Dante is against it
   D. Casey and Dante are enemies and no one knows why

4. Why does Father Dolan whip Stephen during Latin class?

   A. Stephen is not doing his work because his glasses are broken
   B. Stephen is not doing his work because he does not know the answers to the Latin problems
   C. Stephen is talking to another student to get answers to the Latin problems
   D. Stephen is talking to another student because his glasses are broken

5. How does Father Conmee respond to Stephen's request that he talk to Father Dolan about his punishment in Latin class?

    A. He sends Stephen for another whipping

    B. He laughs at Stephen and tells him to return to his dorm

    C. He tells Stephen that he deserved the whipping

    D. He promises to talk to Father Dolan

6. What does Mike Flynn try to teach Stephen to do?

    A. Shoot a gun

    B. Play chess

    C. Run

    D. Write poetry

7. With which novel does Stephen fall in love?

    A. *Frankenstein*

    B. *The Three Musketeers*

    C. *The Count of Monte Cristo*

    D. *Ulysses*

8. To whom does Stephen write his first love poem?

    A. "E—C—"

    B. "R—V—"

    C. "C—V—"

    D. "E—B—"

9. Which two colors does Stephen associate with Dante?

    A. Green and orange

    B. Green and maroon

    C. Yellow and gray

    D. Yellow and orange

10. Which character smokes "black twists" of tobacco?

    A. Simon Dedalus

    B. John Casey

    C. Uncle Charles

    D. Temple

11. Why do Stephen and his father travel to Cork?

    A. To visit relatives
    B. To see the sights
    C. To look at a university there
    D. To sell some things at an auction

12. Why is Stephen embarrassed by his father when they visit Cork?

    A. Simon gets drunk and nostalgic
    B. Simon gets into a fight at a bar
    C. Simon treats Stephen like a little child
    D. Simon spends too much money at the auction

13. What does Stephen do to win prize money?

    A. He wins a footrace
    B. He wins an essay prize
    C. He has the highest test scores in his class
    D. He gives an award-winning Latin oration

14. What does Stephen do with his prize money?

    A. He spends it on new clothes for church
    B. He spends it on books of poetry
    C. He buys presents for "E—C—"
    D. He spends it on his family

15. In what city does Stephen first have sex with a prostitute?

    A. Cork
    B. Dublin
    C. Blackrock
    D. Belfast

16. How does Stephen react to having slept with a prostitute?

    A. He feels proud and serene
    B. He feels alienated and anguished
    C. He feels afraid and depressed
    D. He feels liberated and confident

17. Where does Stephen here Father Arnall give his sermons on hell?
    A. At a three-day Belvedere retreat
    B. At Mass
    C. In class at Belvedere
    D. In the confessional

18. What is Stephen's reaction to Father Arnall's sermons?
    A. He becomes even more alienated and secretive than before
    B. He rejects religion forever
    C. He has a nervous breakdown
    D. He confesses his sins

19. Who suggests to Stephen that he might become a member of the Jesuit order?
    A. The headmaster at Clongowes
    B. The director of Belvedere
    C. Father Arnall
    D. His father

20. What sight makes Stephen realize that he wants to dedicate himself to art?
    A. His beloved on the steps of a train
    B. The performance of a play
    C. A girl on the beach
    D. A group of priests

21. Instead of becoming a Jesuit, what does Stephen do?
    A. He becomes a carpenter
    B. He becomes a doctor
    C. He continues to study at Belvedere
    D. He attends university

22. Which of Stephen's friends at the university is staunchly patriotic?

   A. Temple
   B. Davin
   C. Cranly
   D. Lynch

23. What is one of the basic distinctions of Stephen's aesthetic theory?

   A. Strong vs. weak art
   B. Pure vs. impure art
   C. Active vs. passive art
   D. Static vs. kinetic art

24. Which of the following lists corresponds to one of the distinctions made in Stephen's aesthetic theory?

   A. Prose, poetry, and song
   B. Lyrical, epical, and dramatic
   C. Practical, abstract, and fantastical
   D. Fictional, realistic, and liminal

25. What ceremony does Cranly try to convince Stephen to attend, for his mother's sake?

   A. Christmas Mass
   B. His confirmation ceremony
   C. Easter Mass
   D. The baptism of his younger brother

ANSWER KEY:
1: A; 2: B; 3: B; 4: A; 5: D; 6: C; 7: C; 8: A; 9: B; 10: C; 11: D; 12: A; 13: B; 14: D; 15: B; 16: B; 17: A; 18: D; 19: B; 20: C; 21: D; 22: B; 23: D; 24: B; 25: C

GLOSSARY OF WORDS & LATIN PHRASES

Act of Contrition a traditional Catholic prayer said by sinners who are repentant for their sins

Ad Majorem Dei Gloriam "to the greater glory of God"

in a bake angry

bally a euphemism for "bloody," a British curse

black twist a cigarette of tobacco leaves twisted together

boatbearer a participant in the Catholic Mass who carries the container of incense (the "boat")

Bonum est in quod tendit appetitus "The good is in that toward which the appetite tends"

cachou a cashew mint

camaun a piece of equipment in the sport of hurling; the stick used to hurl the ball

car a two-wheeled horse-driven carriage

catafalque a structure upon which a dead body is laid for viewing

catechism a set of formal questions and answers that sums up Catholic beliefs

chasuble a sleeveless garment worn by a priest during Mass

ciborium a container for the host used during Mass

cock a faucet

come-all-you a form of pub song that begins with the phrase "Come all you..."

Confiteor a Catholic prayer said at the beginning of Mass; literally, "I confess"

constitutional a walk or stroll taken for health purposes

Contrahit orator, variant in carmine vates "An orator concludes, poets vary in their rhyming"

cope   a long semicircular vestment

cassock   a close-fitting, ankle-length garment worn by Catholic clergy

Credo ut vos sanguinarius mendax estis . . . quia facies vostra monstrat ut vos in damno malo humore estis "I believe that you are a bloody liar . . . because your face shows that you are in a damned bad mood."

Davitt, Michael a radical leader of Irish land reform who served time in prison for trying to smuggle arms into Ireland

dead mass a Mass said for the dead

Dominicans a Catholic order of monks who focus on preaching the gospel

drisheen a traditional Irish dish made of sheep's blood, chopped mutton, bread crumbs, milk, and other ingredients

Ego credo ut vita pauperum est simpliciter atrox, simpliciter sanguinarius atrox, in Liverpoolio "I believe that the life of the poor is simply atrocious, simply bloody atrocious, in Liverpool"

ego habeo "I have"

ejaculation a short prayer or exclamation

elements   required classes, such as Latin or mathematics

Et ignotas animum dimittit in artes "And he sent forth his spirit among the unknown arts"; from Ovid's *Metamorphoses*

Et tu cum Jesu Galilaeo eras "And you were with Jesus of Galilee"

false sleeves pieces of material that hung from each shoulder of the soutane, the garment worn by Jesuits

feck   to steal

fender   a guard that keeps sparks from flying out of a fireplace

fenian movement an Irish revolutionary movement

ferule   a flat rod of wood used to punish children; plural "ferulae" refers to the number of lashings a student gets

fireeater   a person who likes to argue

foxing   pretending

Franciscans a Catholic order of monks who focus on asceticism

gallnut   an abnormal growth on a tree

gamecock   a bird bred for cockfighting

gibbet   a structure for hanging

gingernuts gingerbread

glass   a monocle

greaves   shin guards

hacking chestnut a chestnut used in a game of beating one chestnut against another until one breaks *haha*   a fence or wall around a garden that is set in a ditch so as not to block the view

hamper   a basket of food

Hill of Allen a flat-topped hill in County Kildare, Ireland, famous for its memorial to Finn MacCool, a third-century Irish hero

hoardings a fence on which posters and advertisements have been pasted

hob   a shelf by a fireplace

hurling a traditional Celtic sport similar to rugby and field hockey

in tanto discrimine "in so many disputes"

in vitam eternam "into eternal life"

India mittit ebur "India exports ivory"

Indian club a club used for gymnastics

Inter ubera mea commorabitur "My beloved is to me a bag of myrrh that lies between my breasts"; from the Song of Solomon in the Bible

ipso facto "obviously"

Ite, missa est "Go, the Mass is ended"; spoken at the end of Roman Catholic Mass

Jakeen   a lower-class person

jingle   a covered, two-wheeled wagon

Kentish fire strong applause, accompanied by stamping the feet

kisser   slang for "face"

lemon platt lemon-flavored candy

"Madam, I never eat muscatel grapes" a line from *The Count of Monte Cristo* spoken by the hero, Dantès (the count of the title), claiming that he cannot eat any food in the house of his enemy

maneen   an Irish diminutive for "men"

monstrance a container in which the host, or communion, is displayed in Roman Catholic ceremonies

muff a person who is awkward at sports

mulier cantat "a woman is singing"

Nos ad manum ballum jocabimus "Let's go play handball"

novena   a Catholic devotion involving prayers said over the course of nine days

number   a locker

oilsheet   a cotton fabric treated with oil to make it waterproof

pange lingua gloriosa "celebrate with a boastful tongue"

paten   in Catholic tradition, a plate on which bread is placed for consecration

Paulo post futurum "It's going to be a little later"

Pax super totum sanguinarium globum "Peace over the whole bloody globe"

to peach on to tattle or inform on

per aspera ad astra "through adversity to the stars"

per pax universalis "for universal peace"

pernobilis et pervetusta familia "a very noble and ancient family"

pierglass   a tall mirror between two windows

pope's nose the fleshy part of the chicken to which the tail feathers are attached

prefect   a teacher who leads a class or organization

press   a piece of furniture used for keeping clothes

provincial a provincial head of a religious order

Pulcra sunt quae visa placent "The beautiful is that which pleases one's sight"

punch   a hot alcoholic drink

Quis est in malo humore . . . ego aut vos? "Which one is in bad mood . . . me or you?"

quod   "what"

real Ally Dally slang for "the best" or "the real deal"

to redden a pipe to light a pipe

refectory   a dining hall

ripping   slang for "the best"

risotto alla bergamasca an Italian rice dish prepared in the style of the city of Bergamo

rosary   a series of Catholic prayers usually said with rosary beads

sacristy   a room where religious vessels and clothes are kept

sailor's hornpipe a kind of dance popular with sailors

scribbler a notebook

seawrack seaweed washed up on the beach

seraphim the highest order of angels, according to Catholic theology

sick in your breadbasket slang for "sick to your stomach"

sideboard a piece of furniture used for keeping dining items such as tablecloths and silverware

singlet an undershirt

slim jim a strip of candy

smugging a slang term for homosexual play

Sodality of the Blessed Virgin Mary a lay religious association honoring the mother of Jesus

soutane a garment worn by Jesuits

square a ditch or cesspool

stone a measure of mass, equivalent to fourteen pounds

suck a sycophant; someone who follows without question; a brownnoser

sums and cuts math theorems

super spottum "on this very spot"

surd an irrational number

surplice a loose white outer vestment with open sleeves, worn by Catholic clergy

Synopsis Philosophiae Scholasticae ad mentem divi Thomae "Summary of the Philosophy and Scholastic Opinions of Saint Thomas"

Tempora mutantur et nos mutamur in illis "The times change and we change in them"

third of grammar the level of an advanced student

Thoth the Egyptian god of wisdom, learning, writing, and the arts; equivalent to the Greek god Hermes or the Roman god Mercury

three theological virtues faith, hope, and charity

thurible a container in which incense is burned

toasted boss a heated footstool

tram a horse-drawn streetcar

venial sin a minor sin

Vexila Regis "royal flag"

villanelle a poetic form that is French in origin, nineteen lines long, in which two lines are repeated throughout

in a wax angry

Whitsuntide the Christian feast of Pentecost, which occurs the seventh Sunday after Easter

yard a urinal

SUGGESTIONS FOR FURTHER READING

BENSTOCK, BERNARD, and THOMAS F. STALEY, eds. *Approaches to Joyce's* PORTRAIT: *Ten Essays.* Pittsburgh: University of Pittsburgh, 1976.

BLOOM, HAROLD, ed. *Modern Critical Views: James Joyce.* New York: Chelsea House Publishers, 1986.

CONNOLLY, THOMAS E., ed. *Joyce's Portrait: Criticisms and Critiques.* New York: Appleton-Century-Crofts, 1962.

ELLMANN, RICHARD. *The Consciousness of Joyce.* New York: Oxford University Press, 1977.

————. *James Joyce.* New York: Oxford University Press, 1982.

LEVIN, HARRY. *James Joyce: A Critical Introduction.* Norfolk, Connecticut: New Directions, 1960.

MORRIS, WILLIAM E., and CLIFFORD A. NAULT, JR., eds. *Portraits of an Artist: A Casebook on James Joyce's* A PORTRAIT OF THE ARTIST AS A YOUNG MAN. New York: Odyssey Press, 1962.

MOSELEY, VIRGINIA D. *Joyce and the Bible.* DeKalb, Illinois: Northern Illinois University Press, 1967.

RYF, ROBERT S. *A New Approach to Joyce: The Portrait of the Artist as a Guidebook.* Berkeley: University of California Press, 1962.

TINDALL, WILLIAM YORK. *The Joyce Country.* University Park, Pennsylvania: Pennsylvania State University Press, 1960.

A Note on the Type

The typeface used in SparkNotes study guides is Sabon, created by master typographer Jan Tschichold in 1964. Tschichold revolutionized the field of graphic design twice: first with his use of asymmetrical layouts and sanserif type in the 1930s when he was affiliated with the Bauhaus, then by abandoning assymetry and calling for a return to the classic ideals of design. Sabon, his only extant typeface, is emblematic of his latter program: Tschichold's design is a recreation of the types made by Claude Garamond, the great French typographer of the Renaissance, and his contemporary Robert Granjon. Fittingly, it is named for Garamond's apprentice, Jacques Sabon.

SPARKNOTES
TEST PREPARATION
GUIDES

The SparkNotes team figured it was time to cut standardized tests down to size. We've studied the tests for you, so that SparkNotes test prep guides are:

Smarter:
Packed with critical-thinking skills and test-
taking strategies that will improve your score.

Better:
Fully up to date, covering all new features of the tests,
with study tips on every type of question.

Faster:
Our books cover exactly what you need to
know for the test. No more, no less.

SparkNotes Guide to the SAT & PSAT
SparkNotes Guide to the SAT & PSAT—Deluxe Internet Edition
SparkNotes Guide to the ACT
SparkNotes Guide to the ACT—Deluxe Internet Edition
SparkNotes Guide to the SAT II Writing
SparkNotes Guide to the SAT II U.S. History
SparkNotes Guide to the SAT II Math Ic
SparkNotes Guide to the SAT II Math IIc
SparkNotes Guide to the SAT II Biology
SparkNotes Guide to the SAT II Physics

SparkNotes Study Guides: